Children in Clinics

Children in Clinics

A Sociological Analysis of
Medical Work with Children

Alan G. Davis

Tavistock Publications
London and New York

First published in 1982 by
Tavistock Publications Ltd
11 New Fetter Lane, London EC4P 4EE
Published in the USA by
Tavistock Publications
in association with Methuen, Inc.
733 Third Avenue, New York, NY 10017

© *1982 Alan G. Davis*

Printed in Great Britain at the University Press, Cambridge

British Library Cataloguing in Publication Data

Davis, Alan G.
Children in clinics.
1. Pediatrics
I. Title
618.92   RJ45

ISBN 0-422-77370-0

Library of Congress Cataloging in Publication Data

Davis, Alan G.
Children in clinics.

Bibliography: p.
Includes index.
1. Children — Hospital care — Social aspects.
2. Children — Hospital care — Psychological aspects.
3. Sick children — Psychology.
4. Physician and patient.
5. Sick children — Family relationships.
I. Title.
RJ242.D38   362.19'892   82-7841
ISBN 0-422-77340-0   AACR2

Contents

For Gladys B. Davis

Acknowledgements

All writing incurs debts, and conventional acknowledgement in a preface serves as a public and final settling of such accounts. While it is possible to list the people who helped, a mere mention in despatches can never do justice to the amount that is owed them. Nevertheless, I should like to thank Raymond Illsley for his support and encouragement, especially welcome at time of difficult reappraisal of direction in the fieldwork. Gordon Horobin offered help, advice, and consolation in equal measure throughout the project and a debt is owed to him that would be difficult ever to repay. The time of the research passed very quickly, mainly due to my collaborator in the research, Phil Strong. One is lucky indeed to have several years spent in joint work with someone who is a congenial colleague, a good friend, and still laughs at one's jokes at the end of it.

My colleagues at the Aberdeen Institute of Medical Sociology at the time of the project all showed great forbearance in the face of a tendency for all conversation to be reduced to detailed research anecdotes. The other people also funded by the SSRC programme grant 'Objectives and Needs in Systems of Social and Medical Care', especially Heather Gibson, were a continual source of intellectual support and good humour. All of us who worked in 'the Hut' would not forget the unfailing kindness, good humour, and sense of fun of Jeanette Thorn who made collecting typing a pleasant activity. The same is true of other secretaries who have at various times helped on the various drafts and manuscripts, rendering illegible handwriting to elegant double spacing — Anna Tagg, Janice Whittington, Debra Berryman, Dani Rothwell, and Karen Honey.

Thanks are also due to the medical staff who gave us permission to sit in on their clinics and who helped in many ways but cannot be named. Their anonymity hides a great debt of gratitude for the way they welcomed our presence. Hopefully, documenting some of the difficulties of their work is recompense in part.

Our decision to separate the major writing-up of the project was the result of at least three factors: our different interests, the difficulty in compressing a large amount of material into one book, and, the imminent geographical splitting up of the research team.

Some aspects of the project have already been published in papers under the joint authorship of Phil Strong and myself. Phil Strong has also taken some aspects of the project and has prepared a separate monograph (Strong 1980). In it he analyses the general cultural features that are constitutive of encounters between the doctors, parents, and children we observed.

The objective of this monograph is different; it seeks to show the ways in which medical work with children takes on a different character depending on clinic task and clientele. This gives each clinic a distinctive and stable form of parent-doctor-child interaction. The research material on which the two volumes are based is therefore the same but the emphases are different, the one concerned with outlining the general cultural form of medical transactions, the other with the details of variation within the form.

Chapter 6 incorporates parts of a paper prepared by P. Strong and myself given at the Social Science and Medicine Conference, Elsinore, Denmark 1972.

1

The Organization of Medical Work

Childhood today is too important an issue to be left to children. Instead it is a topic of interest not only to parents, but to those countless others who produce works of literature about childhood, to those who write learned monographs about the process of child development and who check children's normality against sophisticated tests, and all those who work in the myriad occupations that chart and document the growing child's progress. Recovery of the world of childhood is an essential aid in most autobiography, a source of fascination in its possibilities for explanation of current character and disposition.

Childhood is a highly valued state, and children proud possessions. The social pressures to produce children have been documented: no 'home' and marriage is complete without them. Collectively, children are held to represent the nation's future, a topic with which people are preoccupied in times of crisis or reconstruction. Not surprisingly, most Western societies have developed elaborate sets of services to secure and guard that future. However, there remains a fundamental tension between collective interests in the child and its future, and the particular interests of the child's parents. The dilemmas that stem from this tension when workers are confronted with neglect, abuse, separation, and illness are not easily resolved, for such workers have the awkward task of adjudicating between the rights of parents in their child and their own performance of the appropriate duties, and the more nebulous rights of society in the child. For example, enough is now known about social variability in child-rearing to dampen the ardour of those who would hastily intervene and judge 'normal' working-class child-rearing practices as 'neglect' (Chisholm 1979). Such occupations as social work, nursing, health visiting, teaching, and medicine do their work in front-line contact with children and their parents. Their work embodies this tension — a responsibility for collective interests, whether they be social, legal, or professional (or all of them) as well as a responsibility for the maintenance and support of parental rights and duties.

In this monograph these tensions will be seen to be present in most encounters between, in this case, doctors and parents and children. The substance of the monograph is to describe the ways in which these tensions are managed in different types of encounters. In the next section of this chapter some of the sources of these tensions are looked at in more detail, as well as some of the ways in which the tension is routinized. It is important to note that children as a category present practitioners with special problems in service encounters. Some of the more general features of these issues are outlined in Chapter 2.

Medical work with children is not an undifferentiated activity. Subsequent chapters look in detail at the ways in which different types of medical work with children are performed and the ways in which paediatric encounters are managed.

Medical Work

Much has been written in medical sociology about the characteristics of doctors, and even more has been written about the characteristics of patients. Surprisingly little has been written about the the doctor-patient relationship and even less about the ways in which medical work varies from setting to setting. Freidson argues that most is an attempt to explain doctor's behaviour by reference to abstractions such as 'ethicality' or to prior medical training (Freidson 1970). Instead, he argues, it makes better sense to look for explanations bearing in mind

> 'that people are constantly responding to the organized
> pressures of the situations they are in at any particular time,
> that what they are is not completely but *more* their present
> than their past, and that what they do is *more* an outcome of
> the pressures of the situation they are in than of what they
> have earlier internalized.' (Freidson 1970:90)

For this reason, a brief review of some of the more general issues that sociologists have discussed in the context of the doctor-patient relationship follows. In it some of weaknesses of previous work are discussed along with some suggestions for ways in which the settings in which doctors' work might impinge on medical practice.

Particular attention will be given to the doctor's role, processes of negotiation, and communication in doctor-patient encounters.

Parsons's (1951) characterization of medical practice as functionally specific, affectively neutral, universalistic, and collectively oriented obscures rather than clarifies some rather important issues connected with medical work. This is all the more important as the actual practice of medicine is not a topic with which sociologists have been overmuch concerned. Their preoccupations have mainly been with factors governing entry to medical care and patients' views of medical services in order to identify key determinants of service utilization. The nature of the work done has largely been ignored with the exception of inferences about the nature of practice gathered from interviews with doctors, or from interviews with users of services.

What sociologists have in the main done is to look at the consequences of medical work without examining the nature of the variations in the content of medical work. Instead, medical work has been regarded as an old battlefield on which David and Goliath are eternally pitched against each other except that (a matter for regret) David invariably loses (see Freidson 1970). The reasons advanced for the loss are connected with the general dominance of the 'professional'. In the face of such a lost cause there is presumably little to be gained by studying the battlefield as we know the inevitable outcome of any battle fought upon it.

However, old battlefields do have their interest, and interest heightened in this case by the fact that the battle is still going on, and that much medical sociology takes as a fundamental premise that its outcome is always in some way to the detriment of the patient. But as Freidson, for example, admits, 'all that doctors do is not the same and does not require the same type of interaction' (Freidson 1970: 316). Thus, we have the recognition that there are several different battlefields, not something that one finds getting due acknowledgement in sociological literature on 'the doctor's role'. Freidson himself, having raised this in the context of the power of the doctor, in 'client dependent' as opposed to 'colleague dependent' practice, lambasts one of the few attempts to typify this variation as indicative of a normative bias in medical writing. Thus, for example, Szasz and Hollander are ticked off, first for being doctors, second for importing professional preferences for different types of interaction into an analysis of 'activity' and 'passivity' in medical interaction, and third for defective logic (Freidson 1970: 316-317).

Yet even Freidson is forced in remedying Szasz's and Hollander's logic to admit that some of his own logical possibilities (especially that of 'passive' doctors) are in fact empirically unlikely or impossible, something that should not surprise him, as the thrust of his whole analysis is that doctors's preferred forms of interaction can be and are routinely adopted due to the overwhelming power of the profession of medicine as a whole. Logically, Freidson should conclude that Szasz and Hollander are in fact correct.

Despite professional dominance, Freidson also allows that 'diagnosis and treatment' might be a hazardous business, particularly when the patient is 'ambulatory' and not completely under the control of the doctor. However, these hazards are quickly overcome by the doctor's deployment of superior 'tactics' for accomplishing the 'task' of 'diagnosis and treatment'. These 'tactics' are taken up and extended by Tuckett in his analysis of doctor-patient relationships which unfortunately has little to say about the different *kinds* of work that doctors do, or about the differences in the relationship between doctor and form of medical organization (Tuckett 1977: 208-10). Instead, for example variations in consultation times of middle- and working-class patients with GPs are often taken as evidence that there are general inequalities in treatment. Perhaps it should be pointed out that, for example, such simple timing procedures are in fact very difficult to interpret simply because they assume that the medical work done is all of a piece, that each diagnosis *requires* the *same* amount of time to establish it, that diagnosis, treatment, and prevention are really all the same thing, and that situational exigencies have no impact on the work done or the manner of its execution (Cartwright and O'Brien 1976). This rather crude approach has to assume that medical work is all the same. Admittedly, the sociological literature on the performance of medical work is seriously defective, fragmentary, and partial. Consequently, it is hard to piece together the ways in which medical work and the setting for its execution together exert a powerful influence on the nature of interaction in medical settings. It is in such circumstances easy to retreat to sweeping generalizations about 'medical work', 'the doctor's role', or 'the doctor-patient relationship'.

Tuckett, for example, elaborates some 'tensions' in the doctor's role which presumably constitute problems that doctors have to manage in interaction with patients (Tuckett 1977: 193-200). These are, briefly, immediate individual needs versus their future interests, allocation of scarce resources, the doctor's work role versus his/her other roles, the interests of the patient's family versus the patient, the doctor's own career interests versus the patient, the state's interests versus the patient, and the failure to cure. These are tensions that are presented as generalized ones inherent in the 'doctor's role'. As a general statement this is fine, but it tends to ignore the different mix in which these might occur depending on the work performed and the setting for its execution. Thus, the extent to which community medicine practitioners are faced with the same problem of the present interests of the patient versus their future interests in Tuckett's terms compared to, for example, a kidney specialist, is surely contingent upon the task, setting, and clientele.

Nevertheless, in Freidson and Tuckett we have at least hints that there might be 'battlefield' management problems for doctors that need exploration, rather than assuming for analytic purposes that they either do not exist, as Parsons tends to, or that they are easily overcome by conscious deployment of superior 'tactics'. Rather, the variation in form of these managerial problems is an empirical question.

However, to typify medical encounters as Tuckett does in extreme Goffmanian strategic terms is perhaps premature. For while there is some evidence that there may be 'negotiation' in some aspects of medical work, particularly the work of Balint-trained GPs who are, in Freidson's terms, to some extent 'client dependent' (though even here in the UK system indirect financing reduces that dependency) in TB treatment (Roth 1963) and in psychiatric interviews (Scheff 1968), it is still a moot point to what extent such negotiation occurs in orthopaedic outpatients, surgery, casualty rooms, routine general practice, and so on, and more particularly, negotiation over what issues (Gibson 1978).

In fact, 'negotiation' as a term has its own difficulties, implying as it does individual purposes that are at variance, desired resources that are distributed so that mutually successful outcomes can only be accomplished through bargaining, and also, as Scheff points out, a shared awareness that it is 'negotiation' that is occurring (Scheff 1968). While these conditions might be met in client-dependent practice, it is difficult to apply wholesale such a formulation to medical practice in the UK. It might be better to see 'negotiation' as a process that doctors allow in some circumstances mainly as a means of relationship maintenance, rather than as fundamental premise in all medical interaction. That is to say, the extent and type of negotiation within medical settings is variable, and negotiation, implying as it does some patient power, occurs only when doctors surrender the right to select issues for discussion or outcomes as negotiable in order to preserve or create a desired relationship. Freidson, for example, argues that second-line medical experts in particular are insulated against patient pressure and are more likely to be preoccupied with 'medical' matters rather than 'social' ones and with satisfying collegial norms rather than patients' demands. Consequently, he argues, little bargaining or negotiation will occur in such encounters when they are compared with those of first-line experts (Freidson 1970: 308). This then becomes a managerial problem for the doctor: when is it necessary to surrender professional power to accommodate the patients' divergent interests? From the literature it would seem to occur over issues that are at best marginal to the doctors' concerns, e.g. sick notes; or where, in Szasz's and Hollander's terms, 'mutual participation' is a normatively necessary precondition for any medical work to be performed at all, e.g. psychiatry; or where long-term patient compliance is required for practice.

A similar deficiency can be found in the enormous literature that deals with the so-called 'problem of communication' that has been of interest to many sociologists (Waitzkin and Stoeckle 1972). The general findings to emerge are that patients are dissatisfied with the communication between doctors and themselves, but, on the whole, seem to like their doctors. Yet here again there are a number of difficulties. The notion of 'communication' is itself usually commonsensically defined in verbal terms and seems to refer not so much to all communication as to the verbal provision by doctors of medically relevant information. Thus, in fact, little attention is paid to other forms communication might take, e.g. non-verbal, or the nature and context of the 'information' received. What is more, the finding of general dissatisfaction is itself never put into processual terms. It is not clear quite what would count as 'good' information for those reporting dissatisfaction or whether there is any generaly satisfactory standard information package that can be identified and translated into ready recipes for doctors to use. For example, does communicating the findings of 'cancer' in a known cancer ward create the same problems for the communicator as communicating 'flu' in a GP surgery? Again, there is a tendency to ignore situational constraints in the literature. Obviously, the provision of information is important, but rather than making the blunderbuss charge of medical incompetence it is necessary to look at the multiplicity of ways in which communication takes place. In evaluating studies of defective communication, attention should be paid to differences in the kinds of communication (e.g. Goffman's distinction between impressions 'given' and 'given off') at different points in illness careers, as well as the situational constraints on the process of 'informing' and 'communicating' (Goffman 1956). It is quite possible that every relationship we have is defective in utilizing its 'full' communicative potential for good reason. Indeed, all relationships in which there are marked power imbalances are probably equally defective. Doctors are probably no worse at it than parents are to children, teachers to pupils, and most professionals to clients in professional consultations. Scheff notes that people are most suggestible when under stress, but illness-generated stress is only one of many (Scheff 1966); there is no reason why communication by doctors should be singled out as so remarkably defective. Sociologists, after all, seem to have earned a certain notoriety for their own inability 'to communicate'.

The emphasis that is placed upon 'communication' in the social sciences probably reflects a humanitarian concern to remedy unsatisfactory relationships, whether in marriage or in the consulting room. Singling out communication as the process to be remedied does not really go far enough, as it is premised on there being a level at which overtly divergent interests can be shown to be mere chimeras. The problem is defined as how to find a way to dispel these fantasies through 'better' talk. However, what is probably more significant is just when the 'need' to communicate in perceived and by whom (Danziger 1978). For the concern with communicating normally arises when relationships are seen as unequal, frustrating, unpleasant, and unjust. In the human relations school of management science we also find a pre-occupation with communication as a solution to the conflict generated by the incompatible interests of management and labour, a substitution of understanding for workers' 'irrationality', and a concern with constructing a comfortable environment for worker and manager alike in which shared goals can be divined and realized. This management approach has not been without its critics. The concern with human relations-type diagnoses in medical sociology probably reflects a concern of sociologists to be of use, as well as a management bias in medical sociology. It results from an assumption that with better talk professional-client encounters will run more satisfactorily. This ignores the differing structural inequalities, power, authority, and resources, that characterize relationships between professionals and their clients. The ways in which these relationships are embodied in particular forms of medicine is looked at in subsequent chapters.

A further feature that has no doubt disheartened people studying medical practice is its seeming individual variability. This is buttressed by the method and rhetoric of clinical teaching, which is highly individualized. Thus, individual clinician variation, which for Freidson means they are not 'scientific' (whatever that means), would seem to defy sociological analysis (and central administration for that matter) which is more at home with overt statistical and social regularities. A further problem is that few sociologists have sought access to such decision making, so we have few, if any, analyses of it except in statistical terms (Bloor 1976). However, these statistical studies in, for example, discharge rates, utilization of therapy, mean length of stay, etc. do show some ways in which medical practice is not completely an individual matter. Instead, work patterns cluster, showing, for example, consistently high referral rates from some GPs as against low ones for others. What we lack to inform us of what such variation means are detailed studies of the work situations which generate such differences, and the ways in which different work situations present practitioners with managerial problems for which, for example, referral is a solution sought by some but not by others (Stimpson and Webb 1976).

So far we have been concerned to point to the uninvestigated features of the work situations of doctors and to the possibility at least that there are managerial problems in work performance despite the 'dominance' of the professional. Why do we anticipate that there will be these managerial problems? As Goffman pointed out some time ago in a rather neglected but prophetic essay, the 'Tinkering Trades', particularly medicine, have moved to 'workshops' where servicing is now provided (Goffman 1961a).

The workshops imply a locale in which the resources, technical means, and personnel to effect repairs can all be brought together in one stable location (Foucault 1973). What is more, workshops are specialized locales in which different kinds of service are available (Waddington 1973; Jewson 1976). Persons seeking service now require either detailed knowledge of which workshop deals with which service or a guide through the labyrinth of services now available. As others have noted, those who work in such places have sets of workshop concerns and priorities as well as their service concerns (Davies 1979). In medicine the itinerant doctor is now as rare as the Hollywood films that immortalized him, even though the associated ideology lingers on. The connections between workshops in a complex division of labour has not yet received much attention, yet it would seem that such divisions of labour have a crucial impact in structuring professional autonomy by limiting what the professional may be autonomous about. Such divisions limit what may be done in particular settings, the kinds of work performed, the types of patient seen, and what constitutes an appropriate referral. Again, they are features of medical work that promote tendencies to stability of practice rather than idiosyncracy.

However, despite these general pressures towards stability there are some reasons to suppose that there will remain some sources of uncertainty in the work performed by the doctor. Goffman notes that the verbal content of servicing contains at least three different components (Goffman 1961b). These comprise a technical one concerned with repair and reconstruction, a contractual one concerned with cost and time, and a sociable one concerned with courtesies, civilities, and deference. Further, the servicer simultaneously confronts a client in at least two different aspects: a social aspect and an 'engineering' aspect. The relationship of the two is potentially a source of tension in service encounters, for issues concerning health and illness often defy such a neat separation. As Freidson and Parsons point out, illness is capable of being classified as both 'natural' (and therefore outside human morality) and 'willed' (in which case it implies either social or individual causation and therefore culpability and responsibility). While illness and handicaps are, from a medical perspective, usually viewed as 'unwilled' and therefore are not regarded as forms of motivated deviance, the fact that they are 'abnormal' or 'atypical' can mean that they are also open to interpretation as results of unreasonable risk-taking or avoidable accidents (Freidson 1970: Chapter II). While these are theoretical possibilities, they do, if they are present in interaction, raise issues concerning the moral status of the interactants.

While for the client the 'problem' is unique, significant, and sometimes extremely precarious in its implications for both the present and the future, from the 'workshop' perspective of the second-line professional such 'problems' are often routine events that present themselves already scheduled, packaged, and preselected by other medical workers. In short, the workshop setting lends itself to routinized methods of management. The division of medical labour is again important as there is not just one workshop, but many. The second-line doctors who work in them do not see each person in order to perform the whole spectrum of medical work, but instead operate within a pre-existing complex division of medical labour. Thus, patients are 'sorted' by the GP before referral to specialist services is undertaken, in which case referral is for some specialist task to be performed, while other 'patients' or 'cases' are generated within the workshops' preoccupations themselves. For example, the Scottish City networks of paediatric services dealt with very different clienteles in different parts of the network. This differentiation of work within the paediatric service as a whole was for a medically generated set of purposes. Each work situation has its own tasks, its own target population, and its own set of problems in managing the potential tensions between the technical and the social aspects of medical encounters. Their work was affected not just by individual medical decisions but a prior set of decisions implicit in the system as a whole (only part of which are the referral decisions of GPs) and the relationship of the workshop to its social context.

As well as the structural differentiation of medical labour, different medical work situations confront different problems in managing the tension between the technical component of medical work and the social. Some are harder to manage than others (Daniels 1969). For example, the assembly line routinization of childbirth described by Rosengren and Devault works well enough provided that the engineering model on which it is premised is not challenged by some other version of childbirth (Rosengren and Devault 1963); when it is challenged by alternatives that stress individuality, 'natural' childbirth, women's rights, and a rejection of the legitimacy of medical control of childbirth, then presumably the *medical* 'management' of any particular childbirth becomes more difficult for the doctor (Danziger 1978). Similarly, the problems of managing a gynaecological investigation described by Emerson (1970) and of managing an illegal abortion clinic described by Ball (1967) are generated from very different circumstances of practice, from social legitimacy or the lack of it, the sex of those engaged· in the task, and so on. In fact, as Emerson points out, there are always problems in medical task management simply because it is not done in a social vacuum but has to pay due attention to the social object at which the task in directed. Where the performance of the task can be done, as it were, independently of the social object then the tension is removed (e.g. as under an anaesthetic or when the patient is in a coma); but even here, unless the state is permanent, some deference is necessary as the patient once again assumes his or her social existence by awakening. Thus, purely clinical encounters are rare. Where patients are used for clinical teaching they are usually asked or informed in advance, however cursorily, so that a tacit social conspiracy to be 'an object' for teaching purposes may exist between doctor, students, and patient. At the other extreme the clinical, social, and moral are inextricably fused and interdependent. In such circumstances the tension will be at its more acute e.g. in psychiatry, so acute that practitioners may here well receive special instruction in *how* to maintain the medical integrity of the encounter in face of clients who define it as a predominantly *social* occasion (Blum and Rosenberg 1968).

In studying the practice of medicine we have to pay attention to a number of features, its sources of stability, tensions in interaction produced by its dual social and technical nature, and the place of work done in an overall division of labour. What needs to be done now is to look at some of the ways in which these tensions may be found in paediatric work in Scottish City.

The division of labour

The place of any particular work setting in the overall division of labour had considerable impact on our doctors' practice. We have argued that the elaboration of a medical division of labour is based on the differentiation of workshops and that these workshops are set up for different *types* of clientele. In Scottish City, as well as an anticipated type of clientele, there was also a 'normal' amount of time allocated to each case. The time allowed was an indication of what medical work *could* be performed. Thus, standard slots of time for clients appropriate to different kinds of task (and incidentally different types of clinic) were made organizationally available. Workshops were characterized by the routine allocation of different standard times of processing the anticipated clientele. These times were subject to assault. While time was set aside and appointments were given, workshop trade fluctuated considerably, not least because bookings were formally done by a separate bookings section in the Children's Hospital. The reasons for this fluctuation lay largely outside any individual doctor's control. For this reason, medical practice in any particular setting was influenced by the *extent* to which the doctor was dependent on decisions made elsewhere in the system for the flow of clients. At one extreme, one might find the doctor completely dependent on others' decision while at the other, a doctor may shape the volume any type of trade to suit his or her own practice preferences. We are dealing by and large with 'second-line' doctors, and consequently 'trade' was structured by *prior* medical decisions in most cases. Nevertheless, as we shall see, different settings faced different pressures induced by differential control over entry to the settings of medical practice.

As well as differential ability to control initial client entry, doctors faced different kinds of constraints in generating their 'own' trade from within their client population. These constraints will be pursued in more detail in subsequent chapters.

Types of tasks

Already embedded in the allocation of different amounts of time within the different clinics was a conception of how long it normally took to accomplish the normal work of the workshop. As well as occupying a different position in the division of medical labour each workshop also had as its primary orientation a differentiation function, a task of sorting the clientele into different categories. While it would be true to say that all were concerned with diagnosis, screening, and assessment and treatment, that is to say the differentiation of their clientele on biophysical criteria of illness, normality, or health and so on, with concomitant elaboration of specific aetiology, intervention, and management of therapeutics or remedial work, what seemed to be of greater sociological importance were each clinic's preferred *social* identities rather than the clinical identities.

Thus, each clinic engaged with a different clientele offered a different array of social identities to that clientele as a result of clinic differentiation. As we noted earlier, medical work does not exist in a social vacuum.

Clinics proffered social identities to their clientele based upon a set of clinical decisions that were not available to either the patient or the parent. Again, this is not novel. For as others have pointed out, a characteristic of diagnostic settings is that they offer the client an identity and often have the social mandate to enforce its adoption, at least for administrative or therapeutic purposes. Scott (1968) talks of the *making* of blind men; Sudnow (1967) of 'the dying'; Macintyre (1977) of 'unwed mothers'; Blaxter (1976) of 'the disabled', and so on. In common with other writers commenting on deviance of a more conventional kind, such as Lemert (1967) Becker (1963), Garfinkel (1956), and Emerson (1969), these authors share a view that organizations that have the work of differentiating a population are not only forced to operate more or less hidden clinical or judicial decision-making criteria, but also by doing so proffer appropriate identities to those they are in the business of differentiating. The whole point of IQ tests is to find both 'the clever' and 'the stupid', and within, say, educational organizations, these 'scientific' designations take on wider social and moral connotations if only because they have different organizational implications for those so labelled (Cicourel and Kitsuse 1963).

What distinguishes these processes and gives them a markedly different flavour is that whereas in, say, criminal proceedings, the 'accused' have the *right* to due process, even if this is more a formality than actuality, the 'scientific' status of clinical and educational differentiation embodies no concept of due process. While the criminally labelled have in theory a right to inspect the evidence, challenge it, and even refute it through the adversary arrangements of court procedures, there is no such institutionalized mechanism for dispute in expert medical and educational decision making. The key institutional difference would seem to lie in different social conceptions of the agent's responsibility for his being subject to the differentiation process.

Typically, adults are deemed socially competent, to know the rules, and to be able to apply them reflexively to themselves and others (McHugh 1970). Children typically are not, with the consequence that the institutional legitimacy of, for example, imputing criminality to children under the age of ten is both open to debate and currently to reform. The trend is to replace judicial processes (where children are concerned), whose emphases are on responsibility, intention, and will, with treatment. This in turn implies non-responsibility, lack of intention and will, and an underlying 'natural' or social cause that can be diagnosed by experts and made available to the transgressor, so that it can be avoided in future. Children, then, are a peculiar category of actors to whom the normal allocation of responsibility is deemed inappropriate. By typifying children in this manner, their conduct is rendered explicable by reference to what we all know children essentially to be like as children, but also to the ways in which they are not yet adults. Different standards apply. Instead, it is the task of experts to investigate essential characterisatics that do not correspond with actual behaviour, and (if possible) to effect a diagnosis and repair (Rose 1979).

Rather than this being a simple clinical process shorn of social implications it is in fact a threatening activity. While, for example, delinquency can be held to be a transitory phenomenon that will vanish once normal responsibilities are assumed in adult life or can by institutional means be 'treated' so that the person does not become a 'delinquent', the issue is seen as at least open to intervention so that disastrous stigmatizing identities can be avoided by treatment rather than punishment. Essentialist views of criminality have perhaps lost their force, at least for the under-tens. But on the other hand, medicine can often be seen as dealing with a set of identities that are still seen in essentialist terms, entities like low IQs and biophysical abnormality.

The task of differentiating actors according to such criteria has profound implications for the essential nature of the child. We are dealing not with epiphenomena that can be altered at will, but with the core of a person's identity which in turn structures all others. In short, medicine deals potentially at least with master status traits that obliterate all others. With their expert status and knowledge, doctors are in a privileged position to legislate on essential normality or essential abnormality. Herein lies the threat that is

implied in all consultations involving young children under twelve
years of age. What might have been spotted as behaviour inappropriate to essential normality may on investigation turn out
to be fully appropriate to a discovered essential abnormality.

We would argue that this tension is present to a greater or lesser
degree in all medical encounters with young children, and
consequently doctors face problems both in proffering these
unpleasant identities and in proffering pleasant ones. For as the
precise clinical criteria are not available to the clientele, parental
doubts can be induced and reinforced in unsuspected ways. Things
left unsaid are as important as what is said.

A word of caution is in order here. As Freidson points out, while
doctors are 'a dominant' profession, their dominance does not
stretch as far as one might think (Freidson 1970). He argues that
while the identities offered by doctors to patients stem from
clinical concerns and are converted into social identities, there are
limits on the power of the doctor to *enforce* the adoption of these
identities. Freidson argues that where in-patient treatment is
performed under conditions approximating to these outlined in
Goffman's *Asylums* there is a greater likelihood of the medically
proffered identity being adopted (Goffman 1961b). But even here, as
other investigators point out, such adoption may be resisted
through the diverse sources of power of lower participants
(Mechanic 1962; Roth 1963; Goffman 1961b). Where consultation is
done on an out-patient basis, the doctor's power is limited to what
occurs in the clinic. Adoption outside the clinic, in the home, in the
community, cannot be enforced and so on; Freidson (1970) and
Mercer (1972) point out that for some conditions the medically
proffered identity becomes a way of life; typically these are chronic
handicapping conditions that are deemed to demand constant
medical intervention and attention and thus form a dominant
identity in terms of which a person's social existence revolves
around the necessity for periodic and systematic contact with
medical staff. Even here, though, the potential for multiple
identities is not eliminated, for contact may be established with
many *different* doctors with the consequence of there being at least
the possibility of patients selecting the identity most suitable for
their own purposes. This is to say that patients are not completely
passive in identity provision and construction.

Clientele

The two major sources of clients in Scottish City were contacts
initiated by clients and contacts initiated by doctors. The former

constituted what we normally consider to be the typical way in which patients reach doctors, while the latter developed from legislative and social concern over the health of all children. While in client-initiated encounters the consultation stems from, at least, initial parental concern with an individual child, the medically initiated contact stems from medically or organizationally generated concerns about the health and welfare of populations. Rather than differentiation being initiated by parents' own concerns as channelled by their general practitioner, the medically initiated contact stems from clinical or organizational concerns to check on the health status of all children, including those currently held by their parents to be essentially 'healthy' or 'normal'. The activity of total population screening suspends that assumption and makes 'health' and 'normality' matters for explicit medical validation. These two stances, which we can call 'receptive' and 'initiative', both have in common the assumption that doubt exists about the health status of the child, though as we shall see later they pose rather different problems in the management of the encounter and the procedures used for the validation of health and normality in the different settings, not least because the 'initiative' stance itself raises a whole set of problems which it then has to resolve. As well shall see, the dominant resolution of these problems takes different forms in different settings.

The receptive stance does not appear to raise any such problems. However, it has been argued that as well as its technical preoccupations, organized medicine is also concerned with social control. Various authors have argued that the work of medicine is not just a curative exercise but is also a form of social legislation. Receptive medicine is not exempt from these charges any more than initiative medicine. Basically, the arguments surround medicine's guardianship of entry to 'the sick role' and its construction of 'the sick role' and 'patient role' as ways of controlling illness as a form of deviance.

Disease is regarded as a moral as well as technical issue with social control being exerted upon ill members of the community to conform to social expectations. Parsons characterizes the sick role as made up of conditional exemption from normal social responsibilities, attribution of non-responsibility for illness, that the state of illness should be viewed as undesirable and the sufferer motivated to get well, and that to do so competent and expert help should be sought (Parsons 1951). While this has been challenged empirically, for example for not covering all types of illness and for being culturally specific, other authors have pointed to the extensions in medicine's mandate as evidence of increasing medical concern with issues that once were characterized as sins or crimes (Conrad 1979). Movements towards total population screening or the provisions of new services for gamblers, child abusers, and kleptomaniacs, as well as the mounting critiques of conventional medicine from the Women's Movement and a general restlessness of clients have led to questioning of the ways in which medicine is involved in large areas of our lives. What seemed to be technically neutral activities were increasingly seen to have social consequences (see e.g. Ehrenreich and English 1979).

Each major type of differentiation presents different problems in managing the medical encounter, for in establishing the health status of the child the doctor is in a number of ways dependent on the child or parent. That is to say, in reaching a *clinical* diagnosis there are all kinds of *social* impediments that the doctor is forced to take into account. As noted before, as well as a purely technical 'component', service encounters also have social aspects which together modify, impede, or facilitate the accomplishment of the technical task at hand. What is argued is that these constellations of social aspects, such as degree of doubt, setting, timing, etc. together give a stability of form to the performance of medical work, and facilitate routinized solutions to the problems that the different clienteles present. Thus, one of the rather striking and, in truth, unexpected findings was the similarity of practice among doctors working in different settings, with one notable exception (who worked in an American city well-baby clinic). Given the rhetoric of individualism, clinical judgement, and even characterological explanations for variation in practice, what was striking was the similarity of practice adopted by different doctors (Strong and Davis 1978).

Problems in task execution

There were a number of ways in which non-technical factors entered into the performance of medical work with children in Scottish City. Some have already been mentioned, namely the overall division of labour which affected the flow of clients, the time available in which to perform the differentiation, the 'receptive' or 'initiative' stance for acquiring patients. There were a number of others that we shall outline briefly here but explore in greater detail in subsequent chapters. There are considerable variations in the extent to which the doctor is dependent on the patient, in this case children, for co-operation and information. If the task of doctors is to differentiate between any set of clinical possibilities in order to typify the child unambiguously in clinical terms, then they are dependent on their clients in a number of ways. To begin with there is the necessity of eliciting an adequate, accurate description of symptoms or signs, an accurate history, and adequate answers to questions designed to confirm or refute possible diagnoses. Where the unit of consultation is a child then there are problems. For children may not understand the correct patient stance in these circumstances, may not define the situation as 'medical', may not 'know' they are ill or even that there is a problem worthy of investigation. Where the children are under five or six there are problems of the existence of vocabulary of a sufficiently descriptive and precise variety that would do full justice to the topic under investigation. Second, in testing children or examining them their compliance cannot be assured. Whereas adults more or less competently surrender their bodies to medical manipulation and examination, perform tests on demand, and comment on sensations experienced, children often cannot, do not, or will not co-operate. Whether this failure is important or not depends on the seriousness of the prior doubt surrounding the child.

Then there are parents. While it has the status of an un-examinable truth in paediatrics that children cannot be considered apart from their parents, this has a good practical basis, though it creates an ambivalence of just which interactive unit has primacy at any particular time, doctor-parent, doctor-parent and child, doctor-child, parent-child. For, if children typically cannot be relied upon as competent members to assume the patient role (let alone the sick role), then someone must assume it for them. Parents or surrogates typically stand in for the child. But there are difficulties with this. Parents are not neutral, detached spokespersons, but are interpreters, and creative mediators of the child's experience. They have a vested interest in the child and particularly that their child should reflect well upon them. Parents then have an interest in presenting their child in a favourable light and, what is more, in presenting themselves as competent parents or more strongly, 'good' parents. Parental memory may be selective or defective; correspondence between lay culture and medical requirements for diagnosis and treatment may be seriously at odds. All of these serve to produce ambiguity about the status of the data presented by parents on behalf of their child, particularly as there is always the possibility that 'the problem' may be parentally produced through faulty interpretation, or even possibly caused by the parents.

Leading on from this is the fact that the parent's version of the child's health identity may be at odds with the medical version. Thus, we noted earlier that where different types of medical identity are on offer in the various settings then there is always the possibility that the parental version may be at odds with that of the doctor. For consultations may be initiated for 'incorrect' reasons, (though in this study the reasons invariably had some prior medical warrant from the GP), and parents may misperceive the medical purpose of differentiation and its social implications. This possibility is perhaps most likely to be present when doubt is induced by 'initiative' medicine rather than 'receptive' medicine. Depending on parents' perception of the identity offered and its acceptability, the parents' presentation of the child will either square with the doctor's version or be seriously at odds with it. Rather than there being a constant overt challenge to the doctor's expertise and organizational authority, opposition or disagreement is likely to manifest itself in competing but co-existent versions of the child's identity.

This should add force to our earlier comment that the literature on medical communication has been skewed in the direction of 'bad' news and verbal communication. For if the doctors have an interest in promoting their version of the child's identity, then there are many ways in which it can be done. The difficulty lies in how to ensure that parents have the 'correct' version, and, what is more, demonstrate they have the 'correct' version. There are also situational constraints; the doctor cannot monitor every occasion on which the child is described and correct it if it is at odds with the medical version. The doctor is constrained in other ways. Communication depends on 'something' existing to be communicated. As Davis points out, while some clinical prognoses are clear cut, others are less so or even ambiguous (Davis 1966). Communication then becomes a hazardous business. Then there are the effects of the encounter itself; if it is an 'initiative' encounter then how does a doctor resolve the doubt that has been created? If it is a 'receptive' one how clear-cut are the clinical signs for either 'good' or 'bad' news? We would argue that each setting with its range of identities 'solves' the problem of communication in rather different ways, invoking channels of communication that are both direct and indirect.

Dependent on the acceptance by parents of the correct version of the child's identity are future actions by the parents in respect of their child. Thus, if a child is 'normal' then no further medical action is necessary or desirable. However, if parents define a 'normal' child as, for example, 'chronically impaired', then future joint action is at best precarious. But should the identity be one that is to be organized around repeated medical contact, then the doctor must ensure that not only do the parents accept the medical version, but they are also prepared to accept their 'proper' role in co-operating with the doctor, ensuring that set treatment regimes are adhered to and better still, actively promoted at home. As noted earlier, doctors are not all-powerful and their influence potentially ends at the clinic doors. If the creation of co-operation and responsibility is of prime concern to the doctor then it has to be actively constructed and monitored through repeat contacts. After all, medication recommended is not always (as others have shown) medication administered; treatment is not always adhered to, and as we shall see, the doctor is not always in a position to enforce his treatment or contact demands.

Further problems sometimes requiring attention from the doctor are the implications of his interest in family life. Normally family life is a private and intimate area legitimately and proscriptively sealed from public view. Hughes (1958) has noted the privileged positions of occupations which have, as a right, access to that privacy, but also the duties of concealing from others such 'guilty knowledge'. Hughes also notes that while such access is a right, it is circumscribed, and delicately and precariously legitimated. Normally such private areas are covered by a tacit rule that while access is available, for example, for doctors, it is only used by consent, either implied or requested, by consultation. Here lies one of the difficulties we noted earlier — the legitimacy of 'initiative' medicine, where invasion of privacy comes from medical concerns and not patient's concerns. How such invasion is clothed is problematic. The legitimacy for investigating private areas is never that clear-cut; it requires both tact and diplomacy for it can reveal material that is discrediting and humiliating for those under investigation. Yet under the scientific rubric of medicine, such areas are legitimate concerns for medical enquiry. Entry, however, has to be granted or invited and not forced. Therefore, for those who hold that such material has a bearing on typifying the child, a mandate to investigate must be sought, trust established, and the *relevance* of such enquiry spelled out. However, to spell it out is potentially to discredit parents' proffered versions of themselves, to cast doubts on the morality of the doctor in violating the trust that the parents have vested in him. Further, relatively harmless questions (from the doctor's point of view) can be posed by the doctor that might be taken to imply moral inspection rather than clinical inspection. Consequently, where differentiation is performed, the questioning of children's competences can be read as questioning the mother's competence and character in raising her children. Such problems once uncovered have to be dealt with, if only for the sake of civility.

The last problem which we raise is that of the limits of medical interest and involvement. As noted earlier, doctors in workshops are part of a more complex division of labour and part of a network of collegial relationships garbed with their own special etiquette. Further, medicine may not be the only profession involved with a particular case. At a lower level, the medical corpus of knowledge may not include a solution to the problem at hand; medicine may fail. Doctors then are faced with problems of managing relationships with other doctors and with other non-medical occupations and organizations. There are then customary limits on what a doctor can do, can influence, and can advocate. Where there are requests from parents that he should act on their behalf there is the possibility that the requests reveal the limitations of either the doctor or medicine as a whole, cause trouble with colleagues by violating clinical autonomy rules, or place the doctor in a position of admitting that he has no control over decisions made elsewhere in the system of health and welfare. An innocent question may then reveal the limits of medical omnipotence.

These, then, are some of the problems faced by doctors in performing their work. We would argue that there are routine solutions to many of these problems and that they occur with differing salience depending on the setting and clientele the setting processes.

These clinical mini-worlds make up a system of medical care. In this case the clientele that the system had developed to service was children. Consequently, some general remarks on children as patients are necessary before I go on to deal with each setting in turn.

2

Children in Clinics

Much of the sociological literature on sick children is concerned with the impact of hospital stays on the readjustment of the child to normal family life, or with the deleterious effects of long-term institutionalization (Hall 1978). Our concerns are rather different. The children observed were mostly out-patients attending different clinics for different medical reasons. Their observed hospital visits were of short duration, even if they continued over a period of years. But, as 'patients', they presented considerable problems. As noted earlier, medical work reaches its 'purest', unfettered form with patients who are in no position to interfere with the purely technical aspects of medical work. These circumstances only occurred in a special nursery attached to a maternity hospital. There, ill new-born babies were separated from their mothers and could, given their age, be treated to all intents and purposes as inanimate objects on which medicine could be performed with no social impediments other than workshop courtesies and rituals.

Apart from these extreme circumstances, children were usually accompanied by an adult, usually their mother, and the medical work performed to greater or lesser extent depended on the child. The less it so depended, the easier the task, for children made poor patients. Indeed, they showed just how good adults were at being patients by comparison. For children breached all the rules that normally govern interaction between adults, and for our purposes, the rules that lie at the back of interaction between doctor and patient. It is not surprising then that paediatricians and therapists whose work is mainly with children stressed the essential, if ill-defined, difference between working with children and adults. Children were not just poor versions of adults, but inhabited a world of their own with its own logic and rules which the worker sought to grasp to make that child's actions sensible (Ariès 1963; Hoyles 1979). But as well as having a theoretic interest in children, workers had a practical one too, to effect some intervention in the child's body should it be ill, and to use whatever material was at hand to work out whether or not such intervention was necessary.

Thus, the normal form of medical encounters did not obtain, i.e., encounters where the patient turns up, competently presents symptoms, answers questions, and helps provide the necessary information for a diagnosis, however tentative. This assumes a background, normal, adult level of competence (Mackay 1973). When it is partially or totally absent, then the performance of medical work has to be tailored to suit the degree of that deficiency. Separation and observation under skilled total surveillance was one answer, while at the other extreme where medical work could not proceed without some active collaboration, elaborate roundabout ways had to be found to accomplish, for example, physical therapy. Even where considerable time and energy was devoted to enlisting co-operation and collaboration it often failed to produce consistently useful involvement. As a result, staff did not bother to seek such involvement unless it was absolutely essential. It proved easier to proceed without it. Consequently, although in a formal sense the child was the 'patient', most encounters proceeded by excluding children as far as possible, relegating them to minor players in a drama whose main characters were staff and parents or surrogates. Such encounters were still hazardous and precarious affairs, for while children were tacitly excluded, they nevertheless were present, and problematic for the main actors particularly as they were not oriented to the encounter in the same ways as the other participants.

This latter point is important, for one of the ways in which to demonstrate competent patienthood is to recognize that some encounters are primarily concerned with medical matters and others not. Children's seeming inability to make this distinction continually raised the problem of their imposing an 'incorrect' frame of relevance upon the events taking place, and by doing so intruding 'incorrect' concerns into the matter at hand. For children lacked the skill to identify that there was a patient 'role' and that they were supposed to enact it. Stemming from that was a corresponding inability to identify a 'doctor's' role and the appropriate rules that guide encounters in which both are present. Children displayed little capacity to recognize what others' purposes might be and to use such knowledge in order to align their own behaviour.

Second, there is the basic raiment of normal, adult conduct with which we clothe encounters of different kinds. Rules, such as those lovingly elaborated in Goffman's work (e.g. Goffman 1978), are complex enough, but again are only background features to interaction. It is the ability to deploy such 'proper' conduct that demonstrates competent adulthood when done to good effect. Thus, one must know both when to be rude and when to be civil and also how competently to remedy such usage if circumstances do not in fact warrant it. Apologies, 'accounts', and all the techniques available for remedying such embarrassing occasions as when we have misdefined or misjudged the situation again demonstrate competence in interaction to produce (more or less) trouble- and conflict-free interaction. Again, these civilities and courtesies that both construct and affirm the reality of particular encounters are not consistently oriented to by children; while they may have have a morally enforceable character, they are from the child's point of view arbitrary, touching and shaping childhood but not generated from within it. Intermittent conformity may be displayed, but not commitment.

Third, there are matters of judgement. Given that purposes have to be achieved, their achievement is not guaranteed without a set of basic tactics for obtaining ends, conscious or unconscious deployment of these tactics, presenting a consistent 'front', judiciously engaging in give and take, the grammars of body postures and comportment. The basic moral recipes with which we accomplish our tasks which involve others are often grossly violated by children by their over-enthusiastic adoption of one to the exclusion of others more appropriate to purpose and setting. The social niceties involved in conversation elude children, for speaking for a purpose is a complicated business, more complicated than speaking for speaking's sake. Medical encounters usually involve conversational skills and proprieties. It is thus important to know just how to introduce a subject, how to select the correct time for its introduction, how to take turns so that each speaker at least appears to achieve their own ends in the conversation, and so on. All these are matters of skill, so deployed that conversation flows naturally, orderly, and fluently and gives due deference to each speaker's choices of subject. Where grave issues are at stake, such skills are all the more important. Not all adults get it right, and almost all children get it wrong.

So far, we have been dealing with general reasons why children are deemed socially incompetent. From this it follows that lacking these basic skills it is hard indeed for a child to turn itself, should ocasion demand it, into a 'patient', let along adopt the complex proprieties of 'sick' role. Such a transformation is a difficult one, implying not just biophysical necessity but also taking the 'sick' role armed with an array of complex personal skills that the sick role and patient role pre-suppose. The children observed during the study demonstrated this incapacity correctly to assume 'patient' or 'sick' roles. They were the reason for the medical encounter and were therefore central to it. Yet despite their centrality they were ill-suited to their star billing. They appeared to know very little about hospitals, doctors, white coats, medicine, the reason for their being there, and certainly about how to be a good patient. This is true for other occupations as well. For example, how does one explain the role of 'social worker' to a child (Holgate 1972; Berry 1972)?

As for the sick role, it was usually of greater significance for the parents to know whether the child was ill than for the child to do so and correspondingly assume the appropriate role. Medical encounters with children as patients therefore seemed to be more concerned with parents' definitions of the child's health status than the child's experience of it.

Children, then, were not expected to know when they were sick, that was a matter for legislation by others. They were not expected to be able to recognize physical or mental symptoms and transform them into likely illnesses, characterized by differential severity, duration, location, or implications for present or future actions. While adults often get it 'wrong' they at least have a stock of knowledge and the right to use that knowledge to seek appropriate remedy. Children, of course, lacked that too, that stock of knowledge available that enables us to abstract and describe verbally physical and mental sensations in a manner which enables others to act as advisers if the issue is to seek 'expert' treatment or not, or how to obtain that treatment from the appropriate expert. Those tasks were conventionally allocated to their parents.

That responsibility was a fearful one. While one has only oneself to blame for not getting one's own illnesses 'right', there is blame to be attached when that responsibility is for others. The weighty responsibility of a doctor for 'his' patients is mirrored by the responsibility which adults have for their children's health and illness, a responsibility not backed with years of training, but with recipe knowledge and practical everyday judgement.

Parents are guardians of a hazardous and unpredictable new product and it is not surprising the extent to which their minute deviations from some hypothetical norm or the kid next door triggers consultations with experts (Robinson 1971). On the other hand, while parents have responsibility for their children's health, working out whether anything is wrong or not is sometimes difficult to do. Davis (1963) in his study of child polio victims notes the way in which more serious implications of initial symptoms were assimilated to a parental belief that children get colds or are off-colour periodically, and that these are self-limiting. Only later, when common-sense explanations of symptoms failed, was expert help sought and ultimately a diagnosis made of paralytic polio. Parents of young children, then, are particularly vulnerable to the stresses of the 'double bind' that Bloor and Horobin (1975) elaborate. For given the general responsibility to seek expert medical care having made a primary diagnosis onself, on entry to the consultation such common sense has to be discarded once the expert takes over. The patient should know enough to get him to the surgery on time, but suspend that knowledge on consultation. While patients are exhorted to present 'early', self-screening is expected by doctors otherwise they would be swamped, with what are from their point of view, 'trivial' illness. When the object of such screening is a child, not competent to do it himself or herself, then this duty falls to the the parents. This responsibility and its associated culpability no doubt forces 'good' parents to inspect their children closely and when in doubt brave a doctor's possible typification of them as nervous 'worriers' (Campbell 1975). This is, of course, buttressed by the statutory surveillance of young children by health visitors, well-baby clinics, school health inspections, and screening sessions, all of which indicate that parents should also be supervised and advised to ensure they are taking proper care and also proper responsibility for their child's health. The only analogous development of services is for ante-natal care. All such services are staffed by 'experts' of various kinds, who have training to enable them to pronounce authoritatively on the health status of children. All competent adults know through experience or folklore how such persons are to be used. People learn that they are to be treated as experts, deferred to even if they are neither trusted or believed, or their instructions are ignored.

Such experts are ultimately the legislators of the existence of health or illness and therefore on the acceptability of illness as an 'account', releasing the individual from normal social obligations. The usual formulation of this process involves an actor capable of making decisions about adopting the sick role and its con-sequences. When children are involved, such decisions lie largely outside their control. These matters are organized for them by others. Children's claims to the sick role are not validated in the same way as adults'. Such claims may be interpreted as 'wrong', 'malingering', or a tactical ploy to avoid obligations. Children's claims are therefore provisional, at best, or disallowed as incorrect and manipulative. For if children do not have the same familiarity with illness as adults, how can they make claims with any validity?

Such claims have to be *agreed* by others or even forced upon the child, restricting play, access by friends, and so on. Again, while the object experiencing illness is the child, the issue seems to be whether the parents *organize* the sick role for the child. It is not just assumed.

A further difficulty with the traditional sick-role formulation is its specification that persons who are sick should be motivated to get well. But while illness is a state to be avoided or to be savoured for as short a time as possible, if the state of illness is not understood then neither can its associated moral imperatives. These again are imputed to or forced upon the child by its parents. In this sense, the child has it done for him.

Bearing all these things in mind it is not surprising that medical work with children and their parents is more oriented to the parents' definition of the child's status than to the child's own and his or her own experiences of illness or health. The younger children observed in clinics and therapy were deemed of such incompetence in matters of sickness and health, and even those of an age perhaps to have grasped some or even all the necessary rules for illness were never encouraged or allowed to display it, at least in clinic contact.

The young, it appeared, shared no wish to get better, assuming of course that they were ill, and knew they were ill in the first place. In the case of 'initiative' medicine they were usually healthy anyway. Children did not overtly voice doubts about their own normality, though their parents might. Children were treated as actors rather like tourists, the mentally ill, or the old, considered to show some human characteristics but to be incompetent in certain key respects. They were never treated as capable of reporting illness, or the lack of it themselves; they did not initiate consultations with second-line experts; they were not treated as capable of accurately describing the onset of symptoms, and were certainly never treated as competent to handle medical instructions or to grasp the full implications of their health status. In short, they were treated as incapable of 'patient-hood', 'the sick role' and 'doctor-patient interaction', at least as sociologists have depicted them.

Herein lies a central problem in work with children, for while we deem them incompetent, one of the key features of childhood to which such work is directed is the extent to which that incompetence will eventually be transformed into competent adulthood. On adult standards they fail and yet we are concerned to assess their potential for becoming adults. The world of children then has to be formalized, graded, and given prospective characteristics, while at the same time the raw material on which to judge these matters is somewhat ambiguous. There is, then, room for competing versions of what that child will become, and even though poor at patienthood, such behaviour as they do display is read for signs of underlying reassuring trends and benchmarks according to which children at different ages can be statistically demonstrated to be typically capable of producing age-graded behaviour at 'correct' or 'incorrect' times.

While medical work, particularly screening, may have an underlying prospective concern, children observed showed little or no concern to demonstrate their competence in this direction or awareness that this was an issue of concern to others. Children seemed more oriented to features of persons and situations in the here and now and not the future. Thus, the issue of what the child would become was of concern to their parents and doctors and therapists, but not the child. Such concern was frequently the apparent motive for seeking expert diagnosis and prognosis. In general, then, children were not oriented to themselves as patients, and were not oriented to medical encounters as a distinct form of encounter with their distinct concern with the child as patient. How then did children conduct themselves in clinics?

Children in clinics

In the special nursery for the newborn there was little or no opportunity for children to interfere with the medical work of either doctors or nurses. The orientation of newborn babies likewise caused no problems on the maternity wards. Children could be washed, fed, cleaned, and made ready by nursing staff for whatever time or task the doctors required with no great difficulty or necessary co-operation from the child. In all other observed settings, children's orientation to the medical nature of the encounter was rather more of a problem in that the accomplishment of medical tasks depended on some degree of co-operation from the child. But, as has been argued, children's orientation to medical encounters was not that of the competent patient. Instead, medicine was done with them to the extent that the child would allow without tearful and disruptive scenes. Even here, though, for injections, blood samples, blood pressures, and x-rays, tearful scenes could not always be avoided. In general, medical work was done to the limits that the child would allow and no further. How hard medical tasks were pressed depended on the degree of medical doubt that surrounded the child.

In clinics children were constrained by the encounter between parents and doctors, but not oriented to it in the same way. Thus, apparently competent conformity should not be interpreted as necessarily implying understanding. It was often more a matter of externally imposed orderliness. Room was allowed for children to indulge in childlike behaviour, but within limits set by the others present. Children had an opportunity to act, but within limits set by whatever was going on between parent and doctor at that time. Children could and did impose their own meanings on objects and events, often meanings totally at odds with what could conventionally be ascribed. Thus, the clinic furnishings constituted for some children a source of interest and even pleasure, while others might attempt to incorporate the doctor into their constructed world. The clinic props were a constant source of interest; not only the toys and books provided, but the telephone, desk flap, the doctor's stethoscope, blood pressure equipment, instrument trolley, the sink, the doors, the chairs, and the weighing machines were demanded as playthings. Anything in the clinic was capable of being turned into a game, a toy, or a playmate (including the researchers), unless some adult cared to legislate otherwise. The limits of such attempts to use equipment or toys were set by parents (never the doctor) who were concerned that their child should show at least some minimal propriety in recognizing that the territory was the doctor's and the equipment for his use alone. Researchers and other audiences, on the other hand, were fair game, as they too were mere adjuncts to the action and not active participants in it.

Similarly, the actions of doctors, parents and doctors, and therapists also had game potential. Testing children is difficult if the rules governing testing are not understood and performance known to be graded in some manner. A request that bricks be stacked (to test and demonstrate motor co-ordination) might easily be transformed into a game where bricks are swapped, dropped, lined up, or even stashed away to be taken as presents. Clapping hands might be required only once, but then repeated in response to all other requests.

The same hazards surrounded conversation. When stories were required they were normally supposed to have some relevance to the matter at hand. Children's stories rarely had this relevance or showed the correct timing. Interruptions were more common than thematic relevance. The stories they told were usually irrelevant or tangential, and often of sufficient obscurity to make the job of decoding them time-consuming and of little direct medical value.

In contrast to the even-tempered character of most encounters, neutral and circumspect in the range of emotions displayed, children often veered dramatically from extreme to extreme;

within a few moments fractious anger could be followed by ingratiating smiles. Others showed no emotion, and some even fell asleep during testing. As well as extremes of emotion, children often violated basic rules of public demeanour. Some were sick in the clinic, others urinated on the doctor, fell floppily about, and displayed runny noses or obsessions with their toes. Adults tend not to do this, unless seriously impaired in some respect. Instead, adults again bring to medical encounters that knowledge and display of decorous behaviour that are part of being a competent adult.

As noted earlier, children acted towards others present in an odd and inconsistent manner. The same child that clutched at its mother for part of the proceedings might suddenly rampage a round the clinic. Shyness or a refusal even to look at others present might be transformed into manic excitement. Some would not speak no matter how hard they were coaxed to do so, only to burst into furious conversation at an inappropriate moment, like the ending of a consultation. Apparent fear of the doctor was as often as not replaced within the session by over-familiarity or improper involvement with the doctor's chair, face, or props. While doctors, relative strangers, were less likely to be the object of the child's attention, the mother was like the audiences, fair game. Here children often exerted demands for attention that were completely at odds with the seriousness of the occasion. It was not uncommon to see a harassed and worried-looking mother coping with the doctor's summary as well as a bored, tired, and over-confident child who competed for her attention. Not surprisingly there was much redundancy in doctors' summaries; after all the mother could probably only hear about a third of it in relative peace and quiet. Where two parents were present one usually policed the child at such serious moments, but when a mother, child, and sibs turned up, the mother was usually at the centre of a competing network of demands for attention and attempts at control. Mothers' bodies and belongings were again used as items for incorporation into some childish project. Not only were the doctors' props at risk, so were the mothers'. More alarming, perhaps, was the unpredictability of just what the child would aim for next. As well as being oriented to the doctors mothers were also usually keeping a wary eye out for the next childish project, its ambitions, its scope, and its likely conclusion. Trouble had to be nipped in the bud, for once out of control, clinic order was hard to re-establish. Thus, a child's escalating demands, if allowed, eventually precluded normal parental control and doctors certainly made no attempt to wade in to medical work with a child on the rampage around the clinic. As one doctor ruefully and wearily remarked on one such an occasion, 'Oh, well, I suppose we'll have to try and catch him first' — and having caught the child, examination proved impossible.

Children paid little attention to the content of encounter between their parents and the doctor. The younger children did not even accord it priority but as something interruptable at will. The older children, while behaving in a more circumspect manner and according it due priority, displayed little overt interest in much of it, sitting quietly beside their parents until called upon for investigation or testing. While parents continually demonstrated their involvement by eye movements, nodding, and verbal assent, their older children did not. More commonly they sat attending to some feature of the setting, like a doctor's squeaking chair or any audience, but in such a manner as to display their lack of involvement in the main encounter. They sat, often looking bored until summoned to the stage to play their part, then to return to waiting in the wings. Older children *were* able to fit their concerns into spaces in the main interaction sequences — for example, asking their mother sotto-voce while the doctor was writing his notes when they would be going home. They had learnt the virtue of silence on such occasions and presumably its associated rewards. The nature of these rewards were not evident in the clinic, but lay outside it in a promise of a trip to a toy shop, a day off school, or the promise of play later. For children, such encounters could not in themselves generate rewarding outcomes, for given that they lacked the motivation to get better or even the knowledge they might be or were ill, such out-patient encounters could not be rewarding occasions in themselves. Doctors were not friends and their freedom was severely limited. The reward for 'good' behaviour lay in other activities altogether.

The management of children in clinics

So far we have been concerned with outlining the ways in which children as 'patients' acted in clinics. How then was paediatric work possible at all? We have already mentioned one major way in which the encounter between parent, child, and doctor was managed, by the routine exclusion of children. This had two features. First, in some cases, where parents were not present, then such children could be treated as purely clinical material without any overt recognition of the child's human status. Their treatment as non-persons spilled over into clinics too in naming practices. Very young children were sometimes referred to as 'it'. Parents however, referred to their children by name, gender or character. Thus, such a reference to the child was usually an embarrassing slip on the staff's part, quickly retrieved by a compliment if possible. Given the routinized nature of paediatric clinics, children often had their names forgotten — 'baby' would suffice to indicate the object of the doctor's attention. Further, given that young children had not yet acquired a stock of different experiences and identities, they were treated by medical staff as much of a piece. Parents might draw finer distinctions but doctors never bothered unless it had some distinct medical relevance.

Second, while recognizing children as persons to be greeted and named, doctors and parents proceeded by unspoken agreement to relegate them to non-participant status. This was only possible with the further assumption that the parents would take on the responsibility both for defining the limits within which childish projects could be undertaken, and for speaking for them as 'surrogate' patients. When no adult arrived at clinics but only a child (only two cases) the encounter was quickly terminated. Such an encounter failed to meet these minimal specifications. As we noted earlier their relegation to minor part players did not always work should children seek to intrude their projects into the main encounter. But most of the time they were relegated to non-participant status, addressed only at the beginning and ending of a consultation, when the parents or doctors tried to make the child 'perform' for the doctor some act to demonstrate a point or elucidate an ambiguity, or to warm the child into allowing a physical examination by the doctor. In some cases, repeat cases, not even this was required and the child would be ignored by everybody. On the occasions when doctors did talk to children it was never about medical matters. Instead, talk was about issues in which it might be felt the child had some interest: school or nursery school, birthdays, dress, toys; or some disarming comments on medical examination items. Thus, the stethoscope would only be commented on as 'cold', blood pressure as 'it won't hurt', or instructions on how to perform particular tests, 'you stand over there and say what I say' for a hearing test. Where the doctor demonstrated what was required, e.g. hopping on one leg the length of the clinic, its medical relevance was never explained, it was merely an odd activity that the child might have some interest in copying. Usually it was not explained to parents either, so quite what parents and child made of it was open to question. While parents might have been able to assimilate such activity to medical expertise and the mysteries of medicine, whether the child shared that interpretation was dubious if only because of the obvious relish with which some children latched on to such 'tests', and

seemed to turn them into elaborate games, the rules of which only
they knew. It was at this point that the doctor's interest parted
company with the child's project. All that he required was a
performance and it did not matter what rules the child imposed on
it as long as it happened (Davis and Strong 1976).

The extent to which children were excluded from the main
encounter varied by age. The under-fives were granted greater
licence by both staff and parents. They were the most
unpredictable, the most variable in their conduct, and the most
incompetent. Their effective exclusion depended on their finding
some other focus of interest other than the main participants. Toys
and books were provided in the clinic, and some brought their own.
If they wished to explore they were allowed to, provided it did
not impede the main encounter by noise or interference with
equipment or by getting into danger (one child attempted to stick
three fingers into an electric socket). Such side involvement
effectively sealed the encounter off from breaches by the children.
One doctor explicitly gave out a toy on the child's entry to the clinic
to distract it while she talked to the mother.

From the age of five and upwards such direct exclusion was not
so actively promoted. Instead, children were expected to be aware
of the primacy of encounter rules. They could still develop their
own projects and explore the clinic but the toleration of disruptive
behaviour was less. Breaches of order brought swift parental
disciplining, for such breaches were held to be 'embarrassing',
implying some minimal responsibility for their action. When, for
example, an energetic child began to dismantle the weighing
machine and run water in the clinic wash-basin these were treated
by parents as matters requiring apology. With younger children
such breaches were a 'natural' hazard, regrettable, unavoidable,
but part of what we all know children are like.

The child's exclusion, however, was never total. Both the younger
and the older ones remained attached to their parents. While the
parents' main involvement was with the doctor, they also gave due
weight to their child's rights in them for attention, succour, solace,
and amusement. Thus, parents, mothers in particular, showed
great skill in managing involvement in the main action and
intermittent attention to their children's projects. Parents readily
played little games with children, held them, made faces at them,
gave them toys and retrieved them when they were dropped on the
floor, all while answering questions posed by the doctor. A
screaming child could be cradled and pacified while discussing,
e.g. medication for epilepsy. Whether in the middle of these
distractions parents heard what the doctors was saying is open

question. Surface assent was usually given and no questions asked. As noted earlier, the redundancy in much of the doctor's summing up ensured some of it would be heard.

As well as exclusion from interaction, or side involvement, more direct means were used to produce some degree of order in the clinic, namely adult authority. As incompetent actors, children were both irresponsible and inferior in status to adults. Children were treated not as individuals in their own right but as part of a pre-existing authority structure. They routinely attended with parents and parents assumed the right to speak for them and to control them. Doctors rarely, if ever, had to ask parents to sanction a child, nor did parents ask for permission to do it. Their right or duty to control in public was implicit. Such a duty was recognized by doctors as burdensome and in some cases of severely mentally and physically handicapped children, intolerable. Nevertheless, it was part of being a good parent to take up these duties, and moreover in an area which the doctor addressed with care and craft. As children were 'owned' by their parents, then what they were like in public reflected on the character of that parent (Voysey 1975). Children are outcomes of parental crafts and skills. To question the child is to question the parents' competence and character. To do this would be to provoke a possible overt conflict and this was something to be avoided if only for its potential for fracturing the relationship. Judgements might be made privately by doctors but never overtly (Strong and Davis 1977). If they were discussed at all it was either at the level of shared experience of the nuisances that children can be, an experience redeemed by the more positive virtues of childhood, or when parents 'confessed' they couldn't cope any longer. Either way, such a discussion would be initiated by the parent and receive a sympathetic response. On only two occasions did parents demand that the doctor do something to control the child and both of these were ignored as inappropriate demands.

Parental authority is potent because of the imputed dependency of children on them, and more importantly the great significance that is placed on the role of the parents in shaping children's lives and providing them with the proper environment for development into secure, socially mature adults. Add the parents' legal rights over their children as well, and one sees the great authority that parents have. This all means, in the absence of any organized oppositon, that families are veritable 'total institutions', within which children reside (Goffman 1961b). The only difference is that children eventually graduate to the rank of 'staff' to produce another institution. Parents then have the right to shape their children, tempered by legal sanctions for doing it wrong.

These rights to shape a child's life are far-reaching even in the most mundane encounters, for parents had the right, and exercised it, to decide what was best for their child, but also as we argued to define the child's experience for it (in this case illness) and structure the child's life in terms of such definitions. Parents in clinic routinely reported what their child had said or done. Implicit in this was a parental interpretation of those events, selective and partial, which was proffered to the doctor. The same held for parents' interpretations of how the child was feeling, the locus of pain (if there was any) and how the child would interpret and react to the doctor's requirements of examination or investigation by x-ray for example. Children were rarely if ever directly consulted on such matters. Mostly both doctor and parent overtly took it for granted that the parents would know all the relevant data and be able to supply it.

Not all parents were reliable surrogates for the child as patient. Fathers in all settings were routinely doubted as reliable informants. Mothers were regarded as more reliable informants on pregnancies, birthweights, feeding difficulties, and child development. In fact few fathers turned up at the clinics observed. That seemed to be a mother's job. Where they did attend, it normally occurred in the setting that dealt with potential handicap. Other 'proxies' were also allowed as reliable informants', for example, grandmothers, fostermothers, and social workers. Those parents with some medical or expert skills, e.g. teachers, were treated as more reliable even if more troublesome. Reliability is, however, a relative matter. It matters on some occasions more than others. Some investigators have found major discrepancies in 'histories' — the issue is whether it matters or not (Wenar and Coulter 1962). Some were totally unreliable. On two occasions when children turned up in clinics alone, they were sent home after desultory questioning and requested to bring their parents with them next time.

The only setting where the assumption was suspended was the one where there was the greatest doubt about the child. The parents' credibility in such cases was more overtly inspected. On the few occasions when children over five were questioned it was unrewarding. Such parental authority was very convenient for the doctor, for when children was questioned the stories they told were incoherent, repetitious, irrelevant, and deeply embedded in a world that the doctor know nothing much about, the interior of a particular family. Parents were better able to summarize, adhere to relevance rules, and provide relevant information that put a particular action in a context of, for example, the family, its frequency and normality. The same process worked in reverse. The doctor's summary diagnosis and prognosis was pitched at the parents, not the child. For if children were to be made to understand, then explanation might take hours. Given a child's limited understanding of the future, the prognosis was irrelevant for them. For them the future would just happen, unshaped as yet by them in any purposive way. Parents, on the other hand, were deeply interested in their child's future, particularly in cases of suspected handicap. But gloomy prognoses would often be kept from them too: such bad news would render the future too horrific to contemplate. So children were never told that they would never walk, or never go to normal school, but at some point their parents might be told.

Another way in which children were excluded from interaction was by the manner in which they were discussed. While for adults some privacy, however notional, is given when intimate matters are discussed, children would be freely discussed in front of them, their character dissected, their sins retold as well as their accomplishments. Such intimate matters are usually delicately handled either by such discussion being done where others cannot hear or by them initiating such a discussion directly with a disinterested professional. To retail your wife's sins, fads, foibles, bowel movements, or lack of grace in front of her to another party is at best embarrassing and at worst demeaning. To talk in this manner about a child in front of them is to demonstrate their exclusion from interaction and to place them firmly in a separate class of actors in front of whom normal civilities would be suspended.

The 'total' nature of the family produced a consultation unit of mother and child where adults' authority was already well established. The basic reason for children's compliance was that the parent demanded it, and that was enough. Questioning of that authority brought swift retribution, either by withdrawal of affection, verbal rebuke, or threats of rewards to be withheld. Greater leniency was extended to the under fives. Their deviance was ambiguously motivated and while reprehensible could also be funny and amusing; yet another demonstration of just how odd children are.

Nevertheless, exclusion and authority do not in themselves produce compliance with seemingly bizarre or boring medical demands. As noted earlier, motivation to get well could not be assumed. Not surprisingly in a series of settings routinely dealing with children, there were a variety of ways in which doctors sought compliance from children to accomplish testing or examination.

Adults adapted their tasks to what the child would allow. Those who could not effect this translation were ineffective. Thus, one horror story was told by a doctor of a membership examination where another doctor was unable to get anything at all from the child and consequently failed. The doctor took pity on this unfortunate and gave him both some hints and some children 'to practice on'. While medical staff were given textbook knowledge about childhood illnesses, development, and personality, the practical skills of eliciting compliance were not taught but were handed on by informal word of mouth, practice, and recourse to more general skills that all adults have to learn in order to deal with children. It was one of the things that made paediatric work very different from adult medicine. Different skills were needed, a liking for children, and greater toleration of disorderly clinics. Some staff were better at it them others (a topic of hospital gossip), and some sought to educate consultants in how to 'approach' a child. One had to know in what order to do tasks to achieve maximum effectiveness. As one doctor said, 'I always leave these bits till the end, that's the things that always upset them', referring to the physical examination. Chocolate drops were available for those being immunized; therapists explained how important it was to work at the child's own height to avoid frightening them; and all staff continually monitored their work, moving on quickly to another task once the child showed signs of distress.

There were five main ways in which compliance was sought. To begin with, doctors or therapists could use indirect measures of pathology. Thus, a doctor might try and engage them in conversation, watched them walking about the clinic, noted their off-stage speech. This produced unwitting compliance, but suffered from the limitation that all that could be observed was what the child did in clinic. A shy, unresponsive child produced no data.

Another means was by attempting to create an intimate friendly environment. The staff would try to work at the same height as the child, to use words and gestures to try and create a membrane round the action so that it was continually focused in a direction useful to the staff. Soft tones, soft touches, and continual praise would be used to gain attention and keep it by continual switching of texts to provide a constant stream of novel experiences. Physical proximity also served to screen out possible distractions, to blot out the audience or parent. All this would be interspersed by comments on the action, on the child's toys, dress or demeanour; jokes were made and shared. The older the child, the more verbal instruction or orders could accomplish these tasks.

Should this fail to produce the necessary compliance then

mothers were asked to take over; the doctor retreated to observe. The mothers often broke in themselves to shortcut the warming-in process, volunteering to take over exhorting a child to 'draw a mannie — where's his head — what goes next — come on, draw the mannie . . .', etc. With shy younger children mothers proved invaluable aides in eliciting responses based on use of more familiar language, expression, and information, and the implied parental approval of a correct performance.

Another recourse was to allow the surface structure to turn into 'play' but unlike play, which has its own rewards, this was 'play' to purpose, and stopped once a particular task had been achieved. There were dangers in using this metaphorical frame; children would become captivated by some and not others: once cube-passing had been established it was often difficult to stop it. Also play implies rules and these were often obscure. Question and answer sessions might turn into sessions where the child merely repeated the question and waited for the next move. In sustaining interaction, though, the game metaphor's advantages outweighed its danger (Davis and Strong 1976).

The final method for producing compliance was brute force. This was easy enough with babies who might object, but could not prevent, for example, testing for hip dislocation, but with older children force meant a fuss. Here, it was important that the medical relevance of force was spelt out, for force usually involved the full co-operation of the mother. Thus, the instruction to hold a child's head tight in order that the doctor should see in its eyes was if anything seemingly enthusiastically carried out by the mother. Such man-handling (with the child's co-operation) was frequent in therapy, and in physical examinations with the co-operation of the mother.

Normal childhood

So far we have concentrated mainly on the interaction problems that incompetent patienthood produces. But in being interactional problems they were also paradoxically indicative of normality or abnormality, health or illness. Individual children who did not behave in a manner that produced these difficulties were suspect, since normal children as a class produced these difficulties. Indeed, it might be the lack of these childish characteristics that brought the child to clinic in the first place. This has considerable importance, for the way in which normality is established is to treat someone as normal. To treat all children as delightful is to confer (potentially) normality upon them. To pay too much attention to a normally excluded child is to call that child into doubt. Thus, by the manner of managing clinic order, normality or abnormality is established. If children are as a class 'spontaneous' 'mischievous', 'explorative', then a child who is not so in clinic is in doubt. Paradoxically then, breaches in clinic order are used to establish children as normal, ill, or abnormal.

The doctor's response to such breaches was indicative of the health status in which the child was cast. To respond to a childish project as a source of amusement is to confer normality upon that child. Should such a project be discrepant with the child's age, then to laugh and joke would be to either hide the truth, to offer the possibility that all will be well, or to be heartless, cruel in delight in another's misfortune. Needless to say, doctors took care to guard against such possibilities.

While children are incompetent, they should show the potential for normal development. Thus, incompetence has its positive side too, showing the child's capacity for development. Children were a source of great amusement in most clinics. Childhood, its incompetence, its happy incongruities seemed to strike staff, parents, and researchers as funny as children mimed the antics of adults, laughed at their jokes or behaviour that led to adult confusion. Of course, children were not always so funny. They could be a penance too but at least everyone present seemed to agree that children were a wonderfully good thing, mysterious beings who showed through their bravura performances the capacity to be normal adults. All this was shown by the responses of doctor to childish antics, pleasure, interest, amusement, delight, in short an appreciation of the wonderfulness of childhood. To fail to respond in these terms was to render the child in medical doubt.

Similarly, parents were assumed to want normal children and it was assumed that parents would cast their children as normal if they could by emphasizing their competence at certain age-graded tests. To turn up and present your child in too discreditable a light was to cast doubt on the parent, not the child.

Thus, rather than simple verbal statements of health status by the doctor, there were multiple channels for conveying the health status of the child. The particular setting, the extent to which children's compliance was sought, the extent to which parental claims were allowed through unchallenged, the extent to which the doctor overtly assented to parents' formulations of the child as normal and treated the child as normal in clinic were of equal, if not greater importance in communicating 'findings'. Each child was measured against what we all know them to be like — for each child was in doubt to a greater or lesser extent and that doubt was confirmed or refuted by reference to what we know all normal 'incompetent' children to be like. Just how this was managed forms the rest of this monograph, for again paradoxically, medical work with children is really work directed at their parents.

3

The Limits of Prevention

The development of initiative paediatric services has taken the form of an elaborate set of services devoted to the detection of medical problems in children at different stages of their development from birth to education, separated from those services traditionally emanating from the dominant consultation model. Perhaps in no other age group does one find such a plethora of medical services oriented to medical surveillance, in this case until the child is deemed old enough to assume responsibility for its own health independently of parents or of entrepreneurial medical services. The nearest analogy is, perhaps, the medical supervision of pregnancy, the course of which is now deemed too serious a matter to leave to the pregnant woman alone (Macintyre 1978).

These features influenced the place of local authority screening services in the network of services concerned with child health. The ways in which clients came to screening, the rights of doctors in patients in such settings together seemed to generate a set of interactional dilemmas for medical workers. These dilemmas seemed to owe some of their character to the fact that the clients were children, but were also influenced by the initiative nature of the medical work undertaken. Many of the features of screening children are then probably features of all initiative medical programmes.

Central administration

In the clinics that were run by the Local Authority Health Department, the individual doctors had no direct control over the patients they saw. Screening sessions were laid on when there were four or more children eligible by age for screening in the area served by the clinic and who would attend by invitation. There was no direct control over who else turned up at the clinics; this depended on passing and unpredictable trade, although the health visitors exerted some influence in encouraging attendances. This they did by advising mothers in the course of routine home visits, as well as by advising mothers who came to the clinic to have their babies weighed, whether or not they should go through and see the doctor over such problems as rashes, coughs, colds, and feeding difficulties. Thus, apart from the semi-predictable screening sessions the clientele of clinics was unpredictable both in volume and in presenting problems.

The individual doctor did not control the flow of work; that was arranged by the central Local Authority medical administration, juggling doctors, clinic sessions and anticipated weekly demand, to ensure full clinics. Doctors were unable and unwilling to use compulsion to get clients to turn up, and could only increase their work-load by using recalls (rare) or by encouraging people to 'drop in' for advice, support or a chat, by tagging an immunization programme to a screening session, or asking the health visitor to remind parents to attend. Thus, the Local Authority doctors were client-dependent, for the doctors were not offering 'primary' care but rather a *community-wide* service that existed alongside another system of care in which parents already had the right to consult their GP, who might also run a 'well-baby clinic' in his practice. A 1969 study reports that of a sample of GPs, 21 per cent had well-baby clinics (Wright 1969). This has no doubt increased since then.

Control over the work-load of the doctor was maintained by the health department administration which monitored the results of screening sessions done by individual doctors, in order either to incorporate them in its 'at risk' and 'handicapped' registers of children in the locality or to arrange health visitor follow-ups of selected children. The screening results were recorded on a standard form that enabled the systematic centralized gathering of compatible medical and social information and its incorporation in the other work of the health department, e.g. arranging health visitor surveillance of 'at risk' children or the removal of children from 'at risk' and 'handicapped' registers. It is worth noting that the criteria of 'risk' were not peculiar to the health department but had been constructed jointly with the local hospital paediatricians. In a check on a random sample of fifty cases from cases seen at hospital outpatient clinics with varying degrees of 'handicap', *all* were 'known' and 'on record' at the local authority health department and under surveillance either via the health visitor network or by local authority doctors.

The screening programme then was highly centralized. Children were 'booked' for attendance in the weeks surrounding their sixth and twelve months of age. Parents would then be sent an invitation to attend, and the clinic would be sent any relevant medical information, e.g. the hospital special nursery discharge summary which was also routinely sent to the local authority health department. As well as centrally provided information, the doctor would also have available the record of any previous clinic attendances as well as the clinics' health visitor records.

The rationale behind total population screening is the detection of illness of abnormality which has either escaped being picked up by other services, or to pick up developmental problems which manifest themselves some time after birth, and to do it on the total population of persons in the age category. While this *total* age grade was the target population there are a number of ways in which it was in practice narrowed down.

To begin with, total population screening was of course only *one* of many medical services. Consequently, there were a number of earlier 'detection' points in the paediatric system and therefore at each of them children were drawn out of the potential 'pool' for total population screening by other clinics or services which instituted their own follow-up systems. The population for screening had already been subject to differentiation. The effect of this was to 'skew' the clinic's population toward the 'normal'. Most abnormalities could be relied upon to have been picked out by other paediatric services. Consequently, spina bifida children, hydrocephalics, Downes Syndrome children, etc. were followed up by hospital services and rarely, if ever, appeared in child welfare clinics.

Of course, in any preventive total population screening such as mass radiography (false positives apart), most would turn out to be 'normal' (Bloor and Gill 1972). But in this particular case the presumption of normality was further reinforced by prior differentiation of the target population. Only the normal remained to be screened, or new arrivals in the area, or others who had not been in contact with prior medical services.

There were some other features which should be mentioned in scene-setting. As we have already mentioned, total population screening was done on medical initative and consequently attendance was voluntary. In fact the take-up rate was quite high, around 80 per cent, while the non-attenders would be followed up through the health visitor system. Nevertheless, attendance for screening was decided by parents and not compelled by doctors.

The screening programme was carried out by doctors employed by the then Local Authority Health Department who, as we shall see, occupied an interstitial position in the total system of medical services for children. A further implication of this was that only part of their work was with children — some were also involved in family-planning clinics and school medical services. Their disposition then depended not just on their work with children but on the administration and allocation of all community health services. Such administration was perforce highly centralized within a Local Authority Department.

From these patterns of work administration stemmed a set of features that were unique to the local authority screening programme, as they operated as a set of general constraints that impinged on every Local Authority doctor's work. These constraints were important features which effectively limited the scope of the doctor's work, particularly where this work was 'educative' or 'preventive' in its orientation.

Before going on to describe the screening work done by the doctor it is necessary to spell out these constraints, for they profoundly affected the work of the doctor and the relationship of doctor and parent.

Clientele

The range of problems presented at Local Authority Child Welfare Clinics were very different to those at the hospital. This was intimately bound up with the ways in which patients were referred within the NHS and the rights that individual doctors had in them at different stages of the referral. Hospital doctors received children by referral either from other hospital doctors (which implied hospital responsibility for the child having been accepted by someone already) or from GPs, where there already existed a brief medical history and a request for its specialist evaluation. The act of referral in these cases legitimately transferred the child from one doctor's care to another.

In both cases the out-patient clinic was the setting in which an evaluation was made whether to hold the child as a hospital responsibility or to refer them back to the GP. Referring back usually occurred when the diagnosis was of a trivial ailment or one that would be better managed elsewhere by re-referral to some other specialist service. This division of care was normative, in that it was held to be the appropriate model by which clinicians should recognize and respect each other's rights in patients. Routine ailments that beset all children were not normally referred to the hospital, as the GP had prime responsibility to treat such cases.

The Local Authority doctor, on the other hand, did not get referrals in the same way. Nor could he or she make them. But they had available to them other Local Authority services that worked on their behalf to exhort parents to attend their clinics, e.g. health visitors, and their work to some extent depended on other Local Authority statutory functions such as housing, education, or welfare. Here again though, the function was usually community-based rather than an individual service, and the doctor's tasks administratively defined. Where doctors employed in the Local Authority did see individual clients they were limited because they could not refer their 'patients' to other branches of the medical services, but had to work via the GP 'suggesting' to him that referral might be appropriate. Therefore, the 'patients' whom the Local Authority got were largely self-referred, generated by the peripatetic activities of health visitors, or had responded to requests to attend sent by the Local Authority Health Department. The Local Authority doctor acted 'outside' the traditional referral network yet had always to 'respect' it. Children were brought to clinics as a result of (i) mother's own decision; (ii) exhortations from the health visitor; (iii) mothers' desire to avail themselves of authoritative validation of their child's normality at a screening session, or for specific services that were known to be 'dispensed' at local authority clinics.

The reasons for casual attendances, then, did not have a medical seal already set upon them, as at hospital clinics. They tend to be concerned with those normal eccentricities to which all children are heir, e.g. mysterious rashes, spots, feeding problems, sudden weight losses or gains, bandy legs, chestiness, discharges, intestinal disorders, variable temperatures, and so on. They embody mothers' concerns about whether these physiological irregularities are worth bothering the GP with, or fall within the normal range for children in frequency or extent. The local authority doctor thus again dealt mainly with 'normal' children for the major part of their casual clinic work. Medical emergencies were very unusual, but clinics had open doors for all who cared to come within the set opening times. Should some condition exceed 'the normal' for young children, then there were limits to what the Local Authority doctor could do, except to seek referral to a specialist via a GP. Some 'casual' attendances were, of course, ill-disguised attempts to check on the adequacy of the GP or other medical service. I shall comment on this later.

The other overt reason for attendance was the request to attend for screening. Even here, though, it was often infused with the mother's other concerns. While 'screening' might provide medical validation of normality, it also provided an opportunity for the mother to clear up any minor questions she might have about the child. The 'screening' session thus, potentially at least, offered the opportunity for many different purposes to be achieved; the mother's concern with getting advice on minor childhood ailments as well as her child validated as normal; the doctor's purposes in developmental screening and education and prevention. As we shall see in practice a meeting for screening in fact tended to be more restricted in its content.

Consequently, where individual service is provided the Local Authority doctor faced a set of problems stemming from their marginality which GPs and hospital doctors did not. The normative nature of the division of medical labour between GP and hospital solved these problems for GPs and hospital doctors but created problems for those who were marginal to it. These problems caused a retreat from active promotion of 'prevention' or 'education', although this ideology was appealed to as a justification for their individual practice. It created instead a passivity in interaction, a concern to avoid interactional trouble, a concern to avoid embarrassment or criticism of 'clients', and a meticulous respect for the division of labour. While this stance might be practical in receptive medicine, its adoption within an initiative mode rendered initiative medicine either impossible or severely limited in practice and possibly ineffective in its consequences. Indeed, some of the concern that surrounds screening programmes is that even if they do detect they may do so in advance of any available means of intervention or cure.

Interactional dilemmas

From these general features stem a set of interactional dilemmas when the doctor was faced with 'patients'. It was important to avoid offending other doctors by appearing to monitor their work. By implication, at least, screening and an alternative 'consulting' service could be seen as both checking and poaching other doctors' work. Local Authority doctors could be seen to be checking that other doctors' work reached an acceptable level of competence, that all was being done that should be done, and that the detection system as a whole was working effectively. They were potentially in a position then to spot mistakes. This might have been acceptable (though it is doubtful) had they been a 'consulting' profession, but their marginality and low professional status made this interpretation of their work unacceptable to other doctors. In interaction with other doctor's patients they therefore took care *not* to offend other doctors or monitor their work even when requested to do so by 'patients'. They commonly backed up other doctor's diagnoses.

The following sequence is a fairly typical example of this taken from a conversation initiated by the mother of a young child. (As in all quoted passages from field notes, the gender of the protagonists and any names have been randomly allocated.)

(D) 'How's baby?'
(M) Says she's not pleased with baby's condition — she has a cold and has been to the GP who told her it was 'just her nose'. M says GP thinks it is trivial but she is still worried.
(D) 'Her nose is *still* blocked is it?'
(M) 'Yes.'
(D) 'Is her chest well?'
(M) 'Yes.'
(D) 'Is she having any treatment?'
(M) 'No — I took her to doctor's when she had her last infection and he thought she was all right then.'
(D) 'We'll have a listen.' (Uses stethoscope on child.) 'Well there's *not* much wrong *there*.'
(M) 'Well maybe it *is* just her nose.'

The topic was dropped at this point.

While screening was done to pick up abnormalities and 'drop-ins' were generally for advice on children's health maintenance, some things required referral. The dilemma that doctors faced was how to effect a referral without causing trouble by insinuating that the patient's doctor had fallen down on his duty or that 'expert' advice was being given to him with the assumption that it would of course be followed. Typically where referral within the Local Authority services was sought it was not a difficult matter, but simply a question of asking the mother to take the child for a further 'check'. But should the condition warrant a hospital specialist's involvement this could only be done via the GP. To protect their relationship with the GPs in the area, to ensure they would 'bear' the occasional 'suggestion' of a referral, the GP's rights in his patients were elaborately protected.

The doctors, when requested by parents, gave 'advice' but never orders, and for 'proper' treatment parents were always told to go to their GPs. Even here, though, there were some difficulties, for advice could always be presented by the parent to the GP as another doctor's firm opinion. To avoid this, 'diagnoses' were never offered. Instead the doctor 'agreed' with the parent that it was of sufficient importance to offer it to the GP for diagnosis and treatment. In some areas, feeding for example, doctors (as well as health visitors) did feel they had the authority to recommend feeding changes. Presumably this was an area in which the doctors felt that GPs would not regard their advice as interference. Feeding was in any case the legitimate province of health visitors and nurses by common medical consent, and of such an apparently trivial nature that GPs would be likely to welcome its exclusion from their own workloads as routine work.

These network constraints invalidated one of the doctor's traditional claims to expertise, the right to prescribe. Local authority doctors were not permitted to prescribe, so that the 'exit ticket' in normal general practice, the prescription, was not available to them. Further, in screening sessions such prescriptions would be inappropriate. This raises the interactional dilemma of what service was being given in exchange for what? In not conforming to the normal 'service' pattern of interaction it was not clear what interactional goods could be exchanged. The authoritative pronouncement of the necessity and benefits of screening in validating normality and detecting abnormality would presumably serve to raise a whole set of parental doubts that were not there before. Not surprisingly, what screening was *for* was never directly spelled out by the doctor. It was just done.

Further marginality was expressed in their lack of contact with any child that they did find to be in need of specialist care. While hospital consultants reported to GPs, no one reported to the Local Authority doctor on the case once it entered the main medical network. This lack of contact was keenly felt by the doctors themselves as a major dissatisfaction with their work.

The absence of continuity of care was also characteristic of Local Authority medicine. While doctors were often attached to only one or two clinics, in practice they were capable of being (and were) moved around according to need. The clinic rooms were multipurpose and used by other doctors and other organizations. In no sense did the clinic belong to the doctors. They were nomadic figures. A child's six- and twelve-month screening sessions might well be conducted by different doctors. The clientele was largely transient, and yet individual services were performed. How then would the doctor relate to his clients?

Physical surroundings

The settings in which local authority medicine occurred were in some cases the antithesis of what modern medicine appears to offer. While one can see a hospital exterior as just an old building it is nevertheless identifiable inside as a hospital. One would have difficulty in identifying some of the Local Authority clinics as 'clinics' at all (a point made by the doctors themselves). Whereas at hospital out-patient clinics one is aware of the resources potentially available, it was not at all clear what resources Local Authority clinics could be seen to have available to them. The clinics were often isolated or incongruously situated like one, for example, attached to a branch Public Library. Others appeared even more improbable candidates for 'serious' medicine by outward appearance and inward furnishing. The medical props associated with hospital medicine were absent, as were the family property aspects of GP surgeries; instead, some Local Authority clinics looked like everyone's property and no-one's responsibility. The medical equipment in some was at a minimum, the furniture was sometimes old-looking or improvised. Some 'facilities' were bad, the people in them often did not look like conventional stereotypes of medical personnel. It was not unusual to see assistants in trousers and bright green overalls. Probably the newest was the 'best' of the clinics and it certainly looked more probable as a 'medical' centre as opposed to another one held in an old, rather run-down community centre. There are also other things to be noted about such clinics. They did incorporate some essential medical props: an essential kit for the doctor of a table, some privacy, however notional, and attendants; a store for vaccines, papers, records; a testing kit-though the physical examination seemed to be done using the doctor's *own* nedical apparatus; white coats were worn.

Morning and afternoon tea was served after the clinic sessions, usually made by one of the auxiliary staff and shared with any other staff who were around at the time. The clinic spaces were any public health doctor's property and were used for many different purposes, e.g. family planning, screening, and other sessions. All in all, the settings worked against any definition of these clinics as places where high-status and serious medical work *could* be carried out. It came down to a doctor in a room with a few props and that's about all. It is also worth noting that Local Authority work was largely done in isolation. Doctors rarely met each other except at meetings in the Health Department; their only 'colleagues' or 'audiences' were health visitors or the occasional trainee nurse.

Doctor-patient interaction

The typical screening session was divided into four main phases. The session opened after welcoming the mother (invariably the mother, in only one case did the father turn up as well) with a set of general questions. The form required details of the pregnancy, and serious childhood illnesses, feeding difficulties, etc. The doctor then checked on developmental milestones at six and twelve months of age. These were supplemented by test items that required the child's co-operation. Then followed a physical examination and a final sequence where any issues raised by the mother would be discussed at length before the mother and child left. The session otherwise ended with a check on immunizations. No large differences in session lengths were observed in the different clinics.

The result of the constraints mentioned above in interaction were such as to produce a relationship between doctor and parent of overt civility and equality. This equality demonstrated itself in a number of ways, for instance in the amount of attention paid to the parents' stated concerns with the child. It was noticeable that whereas in hospital out-patient clinics the agenda was heavily oriented to the presenting problem by the doctor, the 'consultations' in the Local Authority clinics were rather different. Where the agenda was doctor-initiated developmental screening the doctor seemed at pains to accommodate any other concerns that parents had about their children. If parents raised them, even at inappropriate moments, they would be dealt with later. What is more, the doctor would say this explicitly. Also, the doctor paid great attention to these concerns, however trivial, discussing them seriously (rather than legislating on them) before making a carefully circumspect recommendation for action that the parent might take. For example, the following from the opening of a one-year screening session shows how mothers inserted their concerns.

(D) 'And he's getting on fine is he?'
(M) 'Yes.'
(D) 'And you've had no trouble with his feeding?'
(M) 'No he's doing fine with that.'
(D) 'And what about his sleeping, is he sleeping all right?
(M) 'Oh yes.' (C babbles)
(D) (to C) 'He's telling stories does he? What's that story then?'
(D) (to M) 'Has he had any illnesses?'
(M) 'Well, the glands at the back of his neck; I think there is something wrong with them. He's had these spots for the past four days. I think its from his friends. I don't think he's ill enought for measles but I thought it might be german measles . . .'

Discussion of the spots ensued with the doctor saying he would look at them later.

The amount of attention paid to the child itself was considerable in all Local Authority clinics. Even very young children got a considerable amount of attention, praise, and enthusiastic comment. Features of the child's behaviour would be discussed and commented on approvingly, and this would be done in such a way as to validate the mother's pride in her child. The doctor would frequently talk to the child as it did things during parts of the encounter where the mother was being questioned. The child was on stage all the time, all its behaviour relevant and worthy of comment. This can be seen in the following extract:

> (D) 'Could you bring him a bit nearer? Is Alec teething now?'
> (M) 'Yes.' (D gives cubes to C who drops one on the floor)
> (D) 'Whoops! — straight on the floor; does he transfer things from hand to hand?'
> (M) 'Well I don't know really — aye — well he seems to be, he eats anything he touches!'
> (D) 'He puts it in his mouth yes — oh — its gone over.'
> (D) (to C) 'That's *good*, now how about another? Do you want *both* in your mouth?'

This encouraged comments from parents about children's abilities, fads, and peculiarities, which would again be fed back as comments or questions to the child, even if they were rhetorical ones.

Doctors were concerned to prevent 'trouble' occurring at the clinic, trouble that would inconvenience parents, worry them, or embarrass them, e.g. when children were sick, wet, or crying this was treated as an everyday occurrence and the mother encouraged to view it as quite appropriate in the setting. The following extract is an example of this:

Doctor is testing C with cubes (going well)

> (D) 'Here you are have two.' (C is sick) 'Oh — dear.' (Wry smile to mother)
> (M) Laughs and moved to clean up C.
> (D) 'Do you want a tissue?' (Hands one to mother from box on desk)
> (M) 'Thank you.' (Cleans C)
> (D) 'Is he sick a lot?'
> (M) 'No, he's very seldom sick.'
> (D) (to C) 'That's *fine*. Shall I have the brick back before you devour it?' (Produces new test item and moves on)

It seemed that the doctors tried to convey that they knew what children were like and that accidents just happened. They would make comments on how they were going to *avoid* accidents occurring, e.g. during the physical examination by amusing the child or keeping it safely involved. Thus, proficiency in handling children was overtly demonstrated. Such attention *to* the child demonstrated an overt concern with the whole child and the doctors continually presented themselves as people who were friendly, good with children, liked them, and approved of them as a category. There were other reasons for this presentation of self, of course, in that such elaborate courtesies kept child and mother involved in the action and thereby smoothed the encounter into a trouble-free, painless (unless an injection was involved) activity in which mothers could proudly display their children to a professional audience. The warming-in never stopped. They were greeted warmly by the doctor, thanked for attending, and once the session was finished the doctor usually escorted them from the room to collect the next case. Other children present were also always attended throughout the encounter. No child was excluded, no matter how they behaved.

Another notable feature was the lack of medicalization of the clinic. Babies and their problems were discussed in a commonsense way without resort to a technical vocabulary. Descriptions of the child were often in the vernacular, children were 'girnie', etc., and only very rarely did the doctor resort to a technical explanation. In fact, medicine was kept in the background and the clinic often resembled a mother on stage with her child in front of an audience who wore a white coat yet never dressed her actions in a medical vocabulary. No medical comments were offered other than a commonsense description of what the doctor was doing, going to do next, had finished doing.

As mentioned before the reasons behind screening were never spelt out except in very bland formulations, for example 'Now — let's see what he is doing now . . .'. Indeed, parents never asked what it was for. Either they knew, were indifferent, or were perplexed. Whichever it was it did not seem to matter. for the printed form that constituted the kernel of the doctor's questioning was structured so that mothers had only to assent to a whole series of closed questions. A typical opening sequence for a screening session could run:

(D) 'How's Celia?'
(M) 'Just fine.'
(D) 'That's good, and she's a year now?'
(M) 'Yes.'
(D) 'And your husband's fine?'
(M) 'Yes.'
(D) 'And you're pleased with her progress?'

(M) 'Yes.'
(D) 'And she's had no illnesses or accidents?'
(M) 'No.'
(D) 'And can she hold a spoon?'
(M) 'Yes.'
(D) 'Can she use it?'
(M) 'Well she tries ...'
(D) 'Can she drink from a cup?'
(M) 'She tries to do that ...', etc.

The opening sequence of questions were heavily doctor-centred and did not require a story. It was during the examination and test items that there was considerable scope for mothers to give more replies detailing children's interests and idiosyncrasies. The stories told emanated from the mother's observations of normal childhood and were never indicative that they doubted their child in any way. Their medical concerns were more mundane — a rash, a cough, a tummy upset for example were causes of mother's concern and duly addressed by the doctor as minor medical problems requiring 'recipe' solutions rather than sophisticated technical investigation.

The screening sessions were the only appointments. Other cases were worked round them and all were fitted in. All were given time to talk abut their concerns; even when one doctor was once complaining about running seriously late she nevertheless saw a case 'after hours'. This again would seem to indicate that unlike the GP or hospital, clinics were places you could drop in any time it suited you, be thanked for doing so, and receive sympathetic attention.

Similarly, Local Authority doctors seemed more concerned than hospital doctors to give out general advice and reassurance concerning young children, and took this as an indicator of an orientation to health education. However, it was muted and limited in its scope. For example, in this very untypical case the mother had a history of bronchitis and had emitted a racking cough in the middle of the screening session

(D) 'Have you got bronchitis more or less all the time?'
(M) 'Yes.'
(D) 'Do you smoke?'
(M) 'Yes.'
(D) 'Oh well!'
(M) 'But only the *mild* ones.'
(D) 'It doesn't do you any good to smoke even those. How many do you smoke?'
(M) 'About twenty a day.'

(D) 'It would do your bronchitis a lot of good if you cut down.'
    (Switches to examination of child)
Education and prevention were left at this point.

The mother's attempts at care were always honoured as wise and indicative of correct concern for the child's welfare. This was merely topped up by a general advice to 'keep trying' in the case of feeding difficulties or to try a steam kettle for a chesty child; advice was given in terms of likely family-provided resources, for the doctor could provide none of their own because they could not prescribe.

It was noticeable how muted was Local Authority doctors' advice on what to do about children. Even in cases of obesity the doctor handled it with kid gloves, never making a derogatory remark about a child or criticizing the mother directly. All *advice* and guidance was done indirectly by 'suggesting' that the mother 'try' something and if it didn't work come back or see the GP. For example, in this extract the child is very overweight:

(M) 'Is his weight all right for his age?'
(D) 'Well, if anything he's on the big side.'
(M) 'Well, that's what I mean.'
(D) 'I wouldn't worry, he's well covered. In fact he's quite
    plump, don't try to push him to eat anything. What does he
    eat?'
(M) 'Same as we do.'
(D) 'Well make sure you don't give him too many starchy
    things ... sugar ... vegetables and meat and so on ...'
    (Topic switch ending with statement that C is 'Perfectly all
    right for his age'. Mother leaves)
(D) (to me) 'Did you see the *size* of him? I really didn't like to
    tell the mother he is *fat* but he really is. Oh well — they
    seem to like them like that ...'
    When 'fatness' was directly addressed in another such
    case, again advice, not censure, was offered.

Mothers were 'reassured' in their actions, and reassured in such a way as to make them appear rational. When mothers explained what they had tried to cure, and how, then this was invariably honoured by the doctor who supplied merely another recipe to try but never any criticism of the mother's handling of the child.

Local Authority doctors' authority, as noted earlier, was precarious. Given that the clients were voluntary attenders and might vote with their feet, the doctor sought to appear wise, reassuring, and experienced rather than as in possession of a formidable technical competence that did not lead anywhere. To be sure the props were there, the stethoscope, etc., but they were never wielded in such a way as to exclude the parents from the action. Indeed, ways were sought to involve them. Parents were involved in handling the child for the examination, holding it, turning it, steadying it, etc. The parent became an aide. No-one else was in the room but the researcher, and only on a few occasions was he called in to help out, invariably to help the mother to distract the child. The doctor sought other bases for a relationship, friendly concern with the mother and child, interest in family circumstances, and a willing audience to children's performances. The parent did not seem over-awed and did not merely respond to the doctor. In fact, they initiated a lot of the discussion.

A considerable amount of attention was given to the courtesies in the encounter. This concern was shown over any potentially embarrassing subject with immediate remedial work. Tricky subjects were avoided, child-created havoc was defused with laughter. Turn-taking in conversation was consistently allowed in that each party had rights both to raise topics and to talk about them at length. Neither party had exclusive rights to interrupt or change the subject or reject and ignore the other's statements. The mother's rights and concerns in the child were acknowledged, conversation never moved into a purely medical arena where *only* the doctor had rights in it. Thus, parental involvement was encouraged in initiating topics for conversation or in discussing occurrences in the clinic. Switches in the mother's attention were allowed and in the child's. Mother's concerns were balanced by the doctor's 'bits', e.g. the history and examination were balanced by the mother's rights to initiate other topics or suggest some other mode of involvement with the child. Thus, very few gaps or silences punctuated clinic conversations, and the doctor's writing-up was mainly done at the end of the clinic session, not during it, or specifically for the mother in the clinic, e.g. filling in a vaccination card. When such switches occurred they were always explained. Silence rarely fell.

The status of the questions asked and the way in which the mothers' responses were treated showed an assumed reciprocity of perspectives. The questions were never 'technical' but were asked in everyday terms accessible to the mother. Similarly the mothers' responses were nearly always deemed adequate. They were rarely questioned. Even the most indexical questions were rarely spelt out in detail to make sure the answer given 'really' fitted the questions. Mothers' responses were never doubted, at least overtly, and rarely overtly checked by supplementary questions.

In fact, the answers were never in doubt. The most common formulation for questioning a child's competences was to put the question in a positive way so that mothers merely had to assent or elaborate as an answer. Few mothers replied in the negative. The outcome was an overt working consensus in which 'of course' children were doing all they should be doing and there was rarely any question that they might not.

In testing, the child's co-operation was required for a successful session on some items. While most of the items on the agenda demanded minimal child involvement (indeed most could be done on reportage from the mother) or could be tested involuntarily (like hearing and vision), testing motor competencies like stacking cubes, transferring from hand to hand, use of a spoon and cup etc. were problematic. They required the child's co-operation and at six and twelve months of age the child could, and often did, withhold it. This 'failure' to perform as required however did not appear to have serious consequences; children were not 'doubted' for such failure as it was commonplace. Instead 'failure' was remedied by checking with the mother that the child could normally do it and the 'failure' explained away as due to character, setting, or temperament. Such 'failure' had no moral consequence either for they were not of an age to understand that they should perform on demand. 'Failure' then was something for rueful amusement rather than doubt or moral censure.

Other items were checkable in other ways, sitting, balance and standing could be demonstrated by the mother and the physical examination could always be done without co-operation, providing the costs in tears and noise could be borne. Only one physical assessment was abandoned with the child winning and doctor and mother (combined) losing.

The screening sessions then progressed with the doctors demeanour being relaxed and friendly, with much appreciative comment from both doctor and mother, with every indication that all was as it should be and that screening was not to be taken seriously. The issue of normality was never put strongly to the forefront. Instead it was submerged in the business of examining the child and talking with the mother.

Children then were normalized in a number of ways: by the apparent consensus as to their essential normality, the mothers' competence to recognize and report that normality, and the light-hearted manner in which children's incompetence was treated, something for laughter and amusement rather than doubt and disbelief. Mothers' claims were honoured and never contested. It was rare indeed for a mother to 'doubt' her child. Particular rashes or colds might be of concern, but not the child's essential normality.

Local Authority doctors had obviously had a lot of practice with children and had thought out ways in which the child could be brought through the encounter happy, maintaining involvement and avoiding trouble through anticipating it, e.g. chocolate drops on hand for handling crying after injections. Medical activities were sequenced in standard ways to make sure that those most likely to produce trouble occured last.

The doctors continually formulated their practice in such a way as to cover them against any implication of (a) rudeness to parents, (b) rudeness to children, (c) interference in others' treatment, or (d) pressuring parents. Immunization, for example, was presented as an elaborate 'choice' for the parents and what is more, a choice as to whether to have it done at the clinic or by a GP. Advice was given and it was always stressed that it was advice and not a *medically* authoritative statement on what *must* be done next. Often it was phrased as 'What I would do is . . .', 'What you could do is . . .', neither of which were formulation much used by hospital doctors.

At the end of a screening session the doctor rarely had to say how the child had done, for they continually made approving comments on individual items as they went along. When faced with no such direct observational data they resorted to questioning the mother. This, however, was usually reformulated as a question to the child, e.g. (D) 'Does he stack bricks at home?' (M) 'He likes knocking them down.!' (D) 'So you like crashing them, do you?' (to child) 'Is that more interesting? Is it? There you are . . . well, well . . . there's the thing'. This in a sense disarms the question and turns it into a comment on what children are like. Mothers rarely asked whether their children *should* be doing things and the doctor merely said children vary a lot.

The construction of normal children

Local Authority screening sessions, then, were pleasant affairs. The children were presumed normal and typically found to be so. Test items when 'failed' were not regarded as particularly serious but were easily assimilated to what we all know children to be like in public settings. Cues that all was well were continually given off during examination and descriptions of children also indicated their normality. Children were 'cute', 'nice', 'bonny wee things', 'good-natured'; but at the same time were 'handfuls', 'little devils', 'wild' (a local term of admiration) who led their mothers a dance. Such typifications, as we shall see, were more balanced than those of the maternity hospital and follow-up clinic, because doubt was never seriously at issue. Where doubt was expressed by parents it was routinely played down by doctors. Thus, a child not walking at a year was crawling 'cos it's probably quicker', another had a large head 'due to all the brains in there'. Such doubts were attributable to 'normal variation'. Thus recalls initiated by some 'doubt' were disarmed by usually being tagged to very specific items, e.g. 'Come and see me in a couple of months and let me see him walking', and not in terms of a more general concern.

Other problems requiring specific treatment — rashes, sticky eyes, chestiness — were handled by reference to 'recipes' that indicated a knowledge of family circumstances and possibilities. More serious problems that fell outside the doctor's competence were either being dealt with elsewhere or required a referral by a GP to hospital specialist services. Either way, such problems were ones of referral and not treatment. All the doctor could do was to check in the former case and advise in the latter.

In the clinics observed three main types of work were done. First, there was the screening programme, second casual 'drop-in' trade, and third, what we shall call 'body maintenance' work. In the first category of work we have seen that screening as an activity had rather unique features due to its context and its content. The other two types of work to which we devoted less attention conform rather more closely to the 'normal' medical model of client-initiated contact and medical maintenance. These two are premised upon in the first case the client (in this case the mother) recognizing that something is 'wrong' and seeking expert medical advice and in the latter discharging the normal parental duty to avail themselves of immunization against predictable childhood hazards such as diptheria, whooping cough, and poliomyelitis. They contrast strongly with the screening programme. The casual 'drop-in' invites the hidden question 'why are you really here' and invites a story, a history, and an attempt by the doctor to effect a diagnosis. The 'drop-ins' presented the most clear-cut examples of the limits of the doctor's authority. While the style of questioning was more close and detailed, its fruition was truncated, leading either to reassurance that all was well or normal for children of that age, self-limiting and not worth bothering the GP with, or in rare cases involving a recommendation to raise it as an issue with the GP 'to see what *he* thinks'. It is worth noting that for the mothers it did not seem to involve very much worry on their part; they did not appear to doubt the essential normality of the child and nor did the doctor.

In the maintenance cases — invariably vaccinations — the threat to the child's essential nature was again minimal. Indeed, vaccinations were a source of humour to all concerned, except the child. It was a form of medicine that all were used to, its outcome predictable, the awareness of its necessity shared. The only issues were whether the child was fit enough for it and whether any adverse reactions had been noted to previous ones. Once these technical issues were out of the way 'the jab' was administered. Everyone except the child knew what it was for and it had been sought by the mother as a routine service. Both conformed to the normal receptive service model, raised no issues about the child's status and were usually over quickly in five minutes compared to the half-hour set aside for screening.

Screening lacked this service model, its benefits were obscure and were generated from concealed medical concerns and as we have seen, even lacked the possibility of intervention *had* something been discovered to be badly wrong. Talk of children as 'patients' in these three contexts seems incorrect. Patienthood implies the right to treatment and except in the case of immunization it was lacking. 'Sickness' and 'the sick role' also seemed irrelevant concepts. Most were well.

The identities on offer at the clinic reflected this. Normality was presumed and constituted continually and the usual more deferential patterns in medical interaction did not obtain. Instead, routinization of interaction, minimization of failure and in-competence, demedicalization; and a matter-of-fact approach to childhood worked together to continually remove the doubt that screening created. If all was well is there anything to tell? If 'telling' was difficult it was because the message was a banal one — that all was as it more or less should be. Parents were trusted both as reliable reporters and as able to recognize abnormality when they saw it. Good news in this context was no news at all.

The same pattern of deference to 'normal channels' could be seen in the casual trade that the clinics attracted. Thus, one consultation was initiated by a mother whose son had put his head through a glass door that morning. The child had been seen at the hospital casualty department but the mother seemed dissatisfied with their performance. The doctor was faced with a mother checking on the work done at the hospital. After inspecting the child's injuries (taking care *not* to disturb the hospital's work) the doctor pronounced the child fine and to 'prove' to the mother that there was no glass left embedded in the child's eyebrows asked the researcher to come and feel to agree that all was as it should be. Criticism of other services was not countenanced although the doctor assured the mother she was quite right to come if she was worried. The mother's *concern* was correct and laudable though technically incorrect.

The doctor's concern to maintain the relationship was also noticeable in the manner in which some items on the screening schedule were rarely asked and rarely filled in. Direct questions about type of housing, marital relationship (married, single, divorced), or questions relating to the doctor's grading of 'family care' were left unfilled and unasked by the doctor. To ask such questions would have been to introduce what might be seen as moral judgements and moral censure into what was already a difficult relationship without prior invitation to do so. In the same way 'prevention', or 'health education' was difficult to do if only because of the precarious legitimacy that such an attempt would have. Moral reform was rarely attempted, partly because it did not seem warranted but also because of the costs that it would entail — a broken relationship and accusations of rudeness and unwarranted interference. Similarly, 'drop-ins' never came with 'problems' that could be turned into issues of moral reform or censure, because to turn up at all was a sign of 'good' parental concern. Those who came on request for screening similarly had also demonstrated, by attendance, correct moral concern.

A further feature that mitigated against 'reform' was the 'appreciative' stance that the doctors had towards their clients. Attached to the clinics were health visitors who knew their local areas and the families in them over two generations. While suspicious of the claims of the more 'disreputable' families, they nevertheless were able to place idiosyncratic features of family life into a sub-cultural context and in doing so adopted a rather fatalistic approach to wayward families, confirmed by an awareness of the social limitations under which such families functioned, and awareness of their limited interventionist powers. For example, health visitors and doctors told stories of their clients' dubious histories, of the difficulties in working with social workers, of GPs who took over cases from them, and who did not inform the health visitor or doctor about subsequent developments. The two Local Authority doctors most committed to an 'educative' stance were also severely limited by inability to control their clients. Their muted reformist attempts were limited by their inability to follow them through with any direct action. Such action would undoubtedly bring them into conflict with their clients and possibly other professionals or local politicians. Again, the costs outweighed the advantages of such attempted intervention.

This accomodative relationship prevented any likelihood of conflict between doctor and parent and child. However, it also means that attempts to use the encounter to achieve change would be limited. The doctors could appreciate the limitations in

attempting to change individuals in face of long-established
cultural and social forces that produced the background problems
such as poor housing, low incomes, ignorance, and so on. Indeed the
doctors were able to appreciate the limitations of medical
intervention in such circumstances. Rather than advocate change
the doctors generally adapted their intervention to what they felt
was reasonable in the circumstances. For example, homely advice:
to use a steam kettle, they felt, offered a better chance of success
within prevailing cultural patterns than high-powered technology.
Such attempts at change as were made were in the form of advice
from someone who appreciated and understood the difficulties
under which some families laboured. This accomodation results
from a number of things; the marginal position of the service
offered, the uncertain status and legitimacy of public medicine
with individual clients, the presumption of the normality of the vast
majority of clients and the ambiguity of screening itself in raising
doubt where no prior doubt exists.

So the initiative form of medicine practiced in screening, the
marginal position of 'community medicine' with individual clients,
the lack of rights in patients, and the normality of the clientele
together produced a stable form of interaction in the Local
Authority clinics. Children were routinely constituted as normal,
but not by direct verbal means alone. Rather, a whole constellation
of practices together created normal children, such as the form of
questioning, an assumed reciprocity of perspectives, joy and
wonder at children's antics (Davis and Strong 1976; Strong and
Davis 1978). These were grouped in a distinct social form that gave
Local Authority medicine its own unique character.

4

Initiative Medicine

We have noted the hazardous nature of the relationship between Local Authority doctor and client as being due to the marginal position of Local Authority medicine. However, we also noted that the act of 'screening' itself raised the issue of children's normality as in doubt, an issue of obvious concern to parents. As such it was in need of resolution, typically done in the Local Authority settings by continual demonstration of the assumption of normality of the children being screened. We now turn to initiative medicine conducted within a hospital setting. The problems raised by screening are the same, though in this case they give rise to possible client dependency. We shall first look at a maternity hospital's wards and then at a special nursery follow-up clinic to show the manner in which screening was handled.

There are a number of reasons for dealing with these two different settings together as they shared a number of features in common. First, they both occurred in a hospital setting. This has some importance. We have noted that the screening programme conducted by the Local Authority Health Department was done in a context of weak structural legitimation for initiative medicine. The two hospital settings conducted their programmes against a rather different backdrop, one of technically sophisticated medicine organizationally segregated from everyday community services. Hospitals do not deal in trivia, they are places where serious medicine is practiced, where sustained contact might imply some actual or potentially important illness or malformation. In Western medical care systems hospitals, at least in this century, have typically become the repository of a number of key icons of medicine, even to the extent of defining what medicine is. They include the most highly trained medical manpower, arcane knowledge, the most elaborate technical facilities premised upon an engineering model of human disease and its rectification, precise surveillance and monitoring of the course of illness, and availability of specialist services in emergency. Such a disposition of forces indicates the seriousness of the issues that are being dealt with, a theme taken up and amplified in all television dramas that deal with hospital medicine, even where the primary interest may be in the character of the emotional entanglements of the medical participants. Contact with such medical services is unusual and usually dependent on some prior screening by a medical practitioner.

The mode of medicine with children took place in a context which lent it considerable authority. In practice, though, this constituted a source of difficulty in doing screening. For, if it takes place against such a backdrop then the issue that it addresses, children's normality, must surely be more seriously called into question. Again, assuming that many such children will in fact be normal enough then the management and resolution of the doubt created by screening in such circumstances is both more difficult and more important to bring off successfully. We are therefore faced with something of a paradox: greater legitimacy exists for screening, but also a greater need exists to deny its significance.

The hospital and control of work

The extent to which paediatricians could control their workload in the maternity hospital was limited, mainly because the doctors had no control over admissions to the maternity wards, but had to deal with whatever babies were born the night before. Again, the number of new babies varied daily, although the local policy of hospital delivery ensured that there was always work to do, but its daily volume could not be predicted. Thus, the pressure of time strongly influenced the manner in which work was done. To give equal attention to *all* new children would make rounds lengthy and probably impossible in the time allotted for a total round (a morning). Thus, doctors 'shed' pressure by attending to standard inspections of the newborn as their major concern and by relying on nurses or midwives to cue them in to any other problems worthy of attention on the total ward population, ignoring, for example, mothers whose children were being attended to in the special nursery, and using strict criteria for further checks on children where some doubt existed as to their health.

Similar unpredictabilities could be seen in the special nursery attached to the maternity hospital simply because its clientele was the result of many other people's decisions to admit children to the nursery; the paediatrician on duty overnight, the concerns of nurses in the delivery room, and so on. As the clinical eligibility rules were wide, then the potential population for admission was large. Consequently there was continual pressure to discharge children if the nursery was full, for otherwise it meant holding eligible children on the wards. The daily fluctuations in trade and its consequences for the demands put upon other departments, e.g. the haematology laboratory, was a continual source of discussion. However, there were some constraints on admission, namely that the results of, for example, a clinically marginal and 'unnecessary' admission by a night registrar were publicly available for discussion on the special nursery ward round. A further restraint on 'trade' was the liaison function of the paediatrician doing the maternity wards with the nursery. Such liaison gave the maternity ward paediatrician an idea of how full the nursery was and could consequently adjust criteria for admission from the wards. Thus, mildly jaundiced babies might be held on the wards longer as a result. Had the nursery not been full, such children might have been admitted.

Similarly, the special nursery follow-up clinic designated population of all children who had been in the special nursery depended on the criteria of admission in operation at different points in time. Its numbers were also then dependent on medical decisions made elsewhere. From the follow-up paediatrician's point of view the criteria were too wide because such wide criteria ensured that the majority of the population seen in the following clinic were clinically normal. However, the doctor was in no position to change the admission criteria in another part of the system. Consequently, large numbers of children were seen, particularly as the turn-up rate was also high (85-90 per cent) due to the presumed worry and anxiety that parents had about their children. The option open to the doctor to control the work flow was to work quickly, using very restrictive criteria for further recall or review and to discharge the majority of children from any further follow-up beyond the normal ten-month screening.

Standard inspection of the newborn

In the hospital area in which we conducted our investigation the policy was for mothers to deliver their children in hospital wherever possible. The newborn babies were then routinely inspected by a paediatrician for illness or defect twelve to twenty-four hours after birth — a procedure known as 'the standard' — in the course of a general daily ward round by the paediatrician in the maternity hospital. The population inspected was therefore captive, unlike the population attending clinics. However, there were a number of situational constraints that complicated any clinical inspection of a newborn child.

To begin with, that childbirth typically takes place in hospital and is the end process of a nine-month medical surveillance created a context in which the hazards of childbirth were made prominent and childbirth itself a potentially precarious event, for it could only occur under close supervision by trained staff and in a medical setting. Similarly, the attachment of paediatricians to the hospital indicated that these new products might well need specialist care and attention. Things could go wrong and the medicalized context served to highlight the riskiness of childbirth.

On the other hand, the fact of childbirth had no novelty for the institution though it had great significance for the mother. For the mother, assumption of the identity 'mother' was dependent on a successful transition involving the production of a brand new person. The significance of the transition was reflected in the visible ceremonies of flowers, cards, visitors, and proud fathers, and took place in an all-female institution, where these ceremonial aspects were also quite routine. Having survived the initial delivery the child was either put into a special nursery for 'ill' newborn children or kept in the wards by the mother. Whichever happened, the child was subject to continual inspection by trained medical staff. These continual inspections presented formidable problems for paediatricians in conducting them smoothly and without upsetting the mother, especially as the public nature of open wards and the presumed vested interest of the mother in the health of her child, together created a setting for practice which was difficult to manage. Such concerns had already brought about a change in previous hospital policy of inspecting newborn children apart from their mothers. This had meant in the past that the doctor could work to a purely clinical agenda. However, the demerits of this were anxious mothers who feared for the worst and would not believe what the doctor or nurse said when the findings were formally communicated to them. Separation bred suspicion. Instead, inspections were now done in front of the mother, which in effect meant in front of other mothers as well in the open wards.

A further problem in doing the inspection was that it was the first major inspection that the child would have had from a paediatrician since delivery and thus was the first medical statement which established the child as normal or not. Since this was the first inspection the doctor could not presume that all the children inspected would in fact be normal. Rather, some would not despite the earlier decision to admit some children to the special nursery. Thus, clinical doubt surrounded some children, a situation hard to handle in a public setting expressing the hopes of the family for the child. These problems were further compounded by the pressing constraints of the time available to do inspections in a large maternity unit.

The situation was further complicated by the nature of 'the standard' itself. With children aged twelve hours, the clinical concerns of the doctor were largely connected with physical and behavioural normality rather than social/emotional/developmental normality. The inspection was done to identify any birth injury, weight and physical condition (Mitchell 1970). Children at this age 'make reflex responses to auditory, gustatory and tactile stimuli but deliberate purposeful responses are lacking' (Mitchell 1970:212). In this sense children at this age were regarded as clinically asocial, animate objects, and clinical concern was consequently directed at children as bundles of responses to external stimuli. But as we have argued earlier, merely to check such stimuli and responses is not sufficient to constitute the child as normal — clinically normal perhaps, but not socially normal. Herein lies the central ambiguity of 'the standard'. The doctors' concerns are purely clinical or technical yet the doubt engendered by the setting requires more than this to constitute the child as normal. The clash of technical concerns and social demands was most evident in the maternity hospital ward rounds and in the performance of 'the standard'. How a working balance was struck between technical requirements and social requirements was a prime concern to both doctors and mothers. To accomplish the technical task of checking all that was needed was for the child to provide appropriate responses. Yet, to socially constitute the child as 'normal' required the presence of the mother. The 'standard' provided a set of clinical benchmarks to which subsequent development could be fitted. Thus, in reconstructing the medical biography of a child with suspected developmental delay, the early birth and inspection data were of use in establishing the presence of likely predisposing factors for a firmer diagnosis of delay. Technical concerns had to be accomplished if only because of the demand for such records at other points in the paediatric services.

Consequently, the doctors had to find a mode of conducting the 'standard' that enabled them to overcome these constraints, diminishing mothers' anxiety while revealing little, by working quickly while showing appropriate recognition of the significance of the event of childbirth, which addressed mothers' presumed worries without raising new ones or leaving them unresolved. The most common method of doing this was to minimize the *medical* significance of the 'standard' and to present it as a predominantly social occasion. The hidden reasons for inspection, of course, only served to raise worries. The manner in which the standard was done, as we shall see, made it difficult to express these.

One feature which facilitated this was the age of the child and its lack of a biography. Thus, the child was in no position to interfere with the 'standard'. The nursing staff could be relied upon to create good order by having the baby available, clean, and ready for inspection. Also, as the child was a new product the mother had had little time to write anything in one what is essentially a blank slate; it was aided by an available child who could not interfere with a predominantly physical examination and by a mother who would have inspected the baby but would not yet have the data to construct a definitive set of worries. Nevertheless, conducting a 'standard' physical examination was a hazardous business and hospital folklore buttressed this belief.

The doctors routinely employed a number of procedures for handling this potentially fraught social situation while accomplishing the task of 'inspection'.

Indicating normality

Children were invariably greeted as bundles of joy at first meeting, as 'gorgeous', 'beautiful', 'sweetheart', as objects of admiration. Such praise and admiration indicated the desirability of childhood itself rather than any specific feature of that particular child. They were the kinds of description that could be applied by any adult confronting a new baby and its mother, a greeting that indicated a proper respect for the individual mother's relationship with her baby. The greeting was reserved for married mothers — the only unmarried mother seen was markedly *not* treated in this fashion. Instead, the child was kept separately from the mother. Childbirth in this case was a topic for commiseration rather than praise.

This greeting also indicated the focus of the doctor's attention in the relationship, to the child and not the mother. While mothers were greeted courteously enough, little conversation was sought or ensued. The mother's other identities might be the subject of brief conversation but attention was focused on the here and now. The visit was to see the baby. This restricted medical focus also effectively ruled out any parental involvement in the 'standard'. For as noted earlier mothers had little history to present, and any relevant clinical information was in the medical record. Mother's other identities were also irrelevant to the task at hand. The delivery might be alluded to but in terms of commiseration rather than investigation. Thus, the force of the greeting served to separate the object of interest from its surroundings. The doctor was established as 'the baby doctor' and there 'to see baby', not the mother.

This restricted focus was also necessary to take account of the division of rights in the mother and child as a unit. The mother was 'properly' the responsibility of the obstetricians while the child was the responsibility of the paediatricians. Such a division was in practice difficult to sustain over issues such as breast-feeding, which were handled by the paediatrician. These rights in patients may be further confused by the development of neo-natology as a paediatric speciality and its claims for control over the development of the child *in utero*, traditionally an obstetric responsibility. The mother therefore became an adjunct to the 'standard', an observer or audience rather than a direct participant in the main action.

It is interesting then to note that twelve-hour-old babies were systematically talked to throughout the inspection, the main comments addressed to the mother came at the very end, on parting. Also, comments or remarks addressed to the child were an indirect means of communication with the mother. Twelve-hour-old babies did not answer back, but the doctor could nevertheless be involved with them to the exclusion of others around. As comments were made to the child, they did not require or elicit comment or answer in return, which in turn facilitated getting through the inspection quickly. Thus, while one child's cot was pushed close to the mother's bed during an inspection on the grounds that 'She's [mother] the most important person here', in fact it meant that the mother was the most important audience present and not the most important interactant. Indeed, the doctors tended to view 'mothers' as a category rather than dealing with unique individuals. Such an orientation was evidenced in the doctor's general jocular greetings to the whole ward and goodbyes, such as 'Hello, ladies!', or 'Goodbye, light-for-dates mothers'. Thus, not only were doctors dealing with one mother as audience, but potentially, the whole open wardful as well.

In approaching a 'standard', the clinical record and nursing information was readily available, again both features that reduced the necessity to engage the mother in history-taking, or problem-spotting. However, such information was a private matter in a public setting. Nurses and students present were not encouraged to raise clinical problems in front of such an audience. Such matters were the stuff of conversation in corridors, though even this had its dangers for even 'walls have ears' (doctor closes corridor fanlight).

In such circumstances teaching when done had a furtive interstitial aspect that it did not have in other settings.

The clinical world and the maternal world were kept sharply separated. Nowhere was this more evident than in the presentation of the standard to the mother. Its clinical purpose was never mentioned and if described at all was in general terms such as 'a visit to see baby', 'to see how she is doing', or on an occasion when students are present as merely an opportunity for them 'to see the normal ones'. That mothers might have viewed it as problematic was also rarely referred to and if it was, then it was treated in jocular terms e.g. 'don't look so worried, ha! ha! ha!'. Standards were just done and any worries that were produced by mothers were cleared up later on. As mothers and children were captive and the doctor mobile, disengagement was easy, the doctor deciding how long would be spent with the baby. As mothers could not predict this, or the sequence of activities that ended the standard, it was never obvious what was the 'proper' time to raise questions, if any.

Similarly, as the records and nursing staff were important in the preliminary work-up, the mother was unable to gauge the nature of the doctor's interest in the child. As no clinical information was given out, nor any description or rationale of any tests, the mother only had available the demeanour of the doctor to indicate how things might be going. Also, the public nature of the standard probably militated against a mother raising worries or anxieties. In fact, these seemed to be voiced to the nurses in private. Thus, if a particular problem worried the mother it was usually the nurse who brought it to the doctor's attention. Consequently, the setting and agenda worked toward the mother assuming the identity of audience to the doctor's main task of manipulating and inspecting the child. Thus, the public nature of the setting removed many of the potential sources of interference in conducting the 'standard' simply because the whole encounter itself was on stage for the rest of the ward. No one wished to appear foolish in public.'

The doctor's demonstration of involvement with the child also served to narrow the sphere of medical interest. Thus, the significance of the event of childbirth having been alluded to at the beginning of the standard, it was never raised again. Thus, doctors showed no interest in other social aspects of the child than that it was attached to a general class of person called 'mothers' and in no way sought any further information about the mother beyond what situational courtesy demanded. No other identities were relevant; typing the mother was not an immediate problem for the doctor but it could instead be left to the nurses to gather any necessary information on the identity of the mother as a 'worrier' or as exhibiting a problem over feeding. Thus, fathers' and relatives' or even the mother's feelings about the child were just not introduced as possible topics of conversation and investigation.

If they were raised as 'problems' by the mother then they were attended to, otherwise they were irrelevant. Thus, when a mother said her husband was worried about the effects drugs he had been taking might have had on the child, this was taken as a topic of discussion and reassurance. Otherwise it seemed to be assumed all mothers (except unmarried) loved and wanted their babies, that the relatives were delighted by them, in short that the ceremonial affirmation of the joyousness of the transition held in all cases except where tied to specific problems that concerned the child. Brief recognition of it sufficed to stop a host of possible questions.

One feature of the mother that was relevant, but usually in the record, was whether the mother was medically expert or not. A 'wise' mother presented different problems from the uninitiated. One cautionary tale told to a younger doctor was about a 'standard' ineptly performed on the child of an elderly nurse who broke into hysterical tears during the 'standard', fearing a mongol child. The storyteller felt this scene was predictable and avoidable. The point then of the tale was that 'wiseness' mattered. It had to be taken into account in the way a 'standard' was conducted and the way in which appropriate and reassuring information had to be given out and 'given off'. To exemplify this, on one occasion the doctor asked a mother while advising her about breast feeding, 'I'm not teaching my granny to suck eggs, am I — you're not medical, are you?' Also, it helped if you knew in advance whether the parent knew what to expect. Thus, one mother was asked, 'This is your third *candidate*, isn't it?' The mother replied, 'Yes'. Such 'wiseness' was acknowledged by allowing the mother briefly to compare the child with her other offspring.

The 'standard' was performed to a hidden clinical agenda with clinical interest or doubt routinely hidden and sustained by making the mother an audience to it rather than a participant in it. On occasions when the audience showed to much interest in the technical content of the 'standard' as opposed to the cues given off in the doctor's demeanour, such interest was given short shrift, indeed the 'standard' would be presented as lacking in interest. One mother asked some questions about the means the doctor used to measure the baby's length. The doctor said in return, 'Oh, you probably wouldn't be interested in that!' When the mother replied, 'Oh yes, I'm fascinated by all the things you do, but I just wondered why you were doing it. I must have been about four inches long at

birth, I'm so small', a very brief description of the technique was
given and then the subject dropped. To spell out the reason for the
measurement would have been to occasion the doctor to spell out
clinical concerns in what was otherwise a routine 'standard'. The
possibility of something being amiss was thus foreclosed as a topic
of conversation.

Normalizing the abnormal

The 'standard' does have considerable importance as a benchmark
in the records against which subsequent development can be
checked in cases of mild jaundice, abnormal palmar creases, test
results, and so on. At the same time doctors recognized that
children could fool you — a large-looking head might just be
congenital and not indicative of hydrocephalus, children could be
jittery for forty-eight hours after birth so that definitively clear
reflexes may be hard to obtain. Some obvious birth problems can
be transitory: heads can be temporarily skewed, toes temporarily
curled up, hearts can innocently murmur. This then provided the
clinical ambiguity that was central to the management of the
'standard', and the doctors' emphasis on keeping standardized and
accurate records of feeding and weight gain as well as of any tests
performed. Clinical problems might disappear over time.

Thus, while some aspects of the setting could be managed in such
a way as to reduce the constraints on the doctor, the clinical
ambiguity that 'inspection' might uncover still needed managing.

Where such doubt existed, but was not 'obvious', then this would
be passed over until the doubt was resolved by tests or by
improvement over time, for example in the case of the disappearance of a heart murmur. The physical examination of the
child was done using a non-clinical vocabulary and possible clinical
danger points indicated in the 'standard' were given no overt
significance or public recognition but recorded for later use. Thus,
deviation from the normal pattern to talk to another doctor or
student on a more technical manner was presented as 'It's just talk
— it doesn't mean anything', or even routine, for example, 'Don't
worry, we *always* do a bit of talking at this point'.

Similarly, abnormal features of the baby that were obvious but
not be seen as serious were rendered harmless by jokes; thus
curling feet were laughingly ascribed to the child's eventual likely
occupation as a footballer. Such jokes were invariably honoured by
the mother too. Similarly, a derogatory epithet jokingly applied to a
smallish or large child — 'You're a skinny one, aren't you?' or 'My
— you're a *monster*!' — allowed amusement at the state of the child

but did not threaten its normality. Also, transforming involuntary actions with motivational statements put the child firmly within the normal human universe, e.g. to a bawling baby — 'You're exercising your lungs, aren't you, ha! ha! ha!'. The reactions of the child also took on normal human form — 'You don't like me, do you?' (child cries as doctor lifts him). Direct refutations of 'worries' were also made when raised during the 'standard'. For example, on examination:

(D) 'You're small and noisy, aren't you?' (to child)
(M) 'His father's big.'
(D) Measures child — 'You're a *good* length, aren't you?' (to child)

However, some problems are not always so easily resolved or dismissed. Thus, while many children were at the end of the 'standard' defined as 'first class', 'fine', 'a super baby', a minority were only 'all right at the moment', leaving open the possibility of something emerging later on during the child's stay in hospital. Where the mother managed to ask a question that raised doubt about the child once the 'standard' had revealed nothing of note, the typification of the child by the doctor invariably employed hyperbole. Thus, one child was described as 'in first-class condition' and another as 'perfect'. The mother's expression of doubt called out strong refutations from the doctor.

On subsequent ward rounds the amount of attention a child received seemed to depend on the degree of doubt that surrounded the child. Thus, one child with abnormal palmar creases that could have been indicative of mongolism seemed to be regularly 'checked' on each ward round, as was the mother, in case it turned out to be some minor congenital abnormality. When the mother asked why this checking was always being done, all she was told was, 'We just like to check these things'. 'Has the Guthrie (a test for phenylketonuria) been done?' Mother replied, 'No'. Doctor said, 'Fine' (leaves room). Tests were not explained except on one occasion when a mother had directly asked and then she was told, 'No news is good news', in a cheery fashion. Other children on the wards were largely ignored if no problem had been uncovered by the 'standard', if no problem had been spotted by nursing staff, and if the mother was reacting to the child properly and treating the child as normal.

Where the doctor checked a child exhibiting something wrong that was visible to the mother than that would indicate abnormality, the doctor stressed that such problems were quite normal or even predictable. All that was required was surveillance for, for example, mild jaundice, which at worst would mean the child going off to 'sunbathe' under phototherapy. On the other hand, children returned to mothers from special nursery were singled out for special attention, emphasizing that the problem was now well past. Others present might be invoked to buttress such appeals to normality. Thus, one child returned by a nurse to its mother from the special nursery after jaundice was greeted by the doctor as a success story, particularly as he was gaining weight well.

(D) 'And *everyone's* happy with him?'
(N) 'Yes.'
(D) 'So that's *two* success stories, then, isn't it?'
(M) 'Yes' (proudly).

The doctor was equally emphatic about a child suspected of having pyloric stenosis, saying finally, 'Well, the x-rays are perfectly all right so he's *fine* — so that's you *both* for the road now!' (i.e. discharge from hospital).

Other visible problems were *trivialized* — in a case of a headspot the doctor laughed, looked askance at the mother and said to the child — 'It's all right, baby's *allowed* to have those!' In such cases mothers' worries could be laughed at directly as peculiarities were uncovered. For example, when confronted with a large baby and a worried mother, the doctor laughed and said, 'I think he's going to be seven feet tall' (everyone round bed laughs). Such trivialization of deviations was common if only because the problems themselves were so common. Few babies were born that perfect; spots and sticky eyes were routine enough occurrences in general, though not for a particular mother.

Even more serious defects did not stop children being described as 'gorgeous'. Mock threats also served to indicate the relative normality of the abnormal. Thus, a mother worried by having a child with extra toes who had expressed her concern to a nurse who passed it on to the doctor was jocularly addressed in a mocking fashion, 'He's got the right ration of fingers, hasn't he? You don't *want* us to find anything else, do you?' This rather heavy humour silenced the mother when followed up with a detailed explanation of how such things were not so uncommon and, indeed, were quite 'normal'.

Such obvious abnormalities as cleft palates, extra toes, injured feet, did not impair the child's essential normality. Rather, there were developed medical procedures for managing these. While such children could still be described in glowing terms, they manifestly had something wrong with them. Appeals to normality alone were not enough. Instead, other tactics were used to cope with the anxious mother, one that was normally played down by the doctor, namely medical expertise and authority. In such cases other experts were invoked who would, for example, do 'a good repair job' on a cleft palate. Not only were such cases relatively normal pathology and therefore not very serious, but also there were well-developed surgical and medical techniques or services that would swing into remedial action at the appropriate time. Yet having invoked the clinical world of medicine, parental competence was always stressed, a competence which when combined with skilled medical intervention would correct the obvious deformities. Mothers were told they could, and implicitly should, cope once the mother and child were out of hospital.

As well as being able to invoke specialist aid the doctor was also able to invoke supportive services that would continue giving advice and also surveillance. Thus, letters to GPs and health visitors were promised and consequent support until corrective treatment would be undertaken. Meanwhile, the doctor was able to give instructions on, for example, mobilizing limbs, treating sticky eyes, and feeding from a background of invoked medical knowledge. In addition the doctor was able to use clinical expertise to minimize clinical interest of odd features like extra toes. They were of sufficient unimportance to be shrugged off as clinically 'quite routine' from a medical perspective though, of course, from a parental viewpoint they are unique. Thus, recipes about how shoes could easily be obtained for such children indicated the existence of a world where such phenomena were quite routine, normal, and manageable. The clinical pronouncements placed the child firmly within the normal category, they were in no way to be seen as indicative of an 'abnormal' child. They were still 'gorgeous' children with 'beautiful leggies', children their mothers could still be proud of.

Discharging: the special nursery follow-up clinic

The clinic attached to the special nursery carried out a routine follow-up of all cases that had been on the special nursery at birth and were 'at risk', if necessary to eighteen months of age when they were transferred to the local children's hospital for follow-up. It therefore dealt with past illnesses and current performances, working from a standard schedule and seeing cases at ten-minute intervals. A typical clinic loading was eight or nine children a session. Given the wide criteria for admission to the nursery a large number (all except two) out of twenty-seven cases seen at the clinic at ten months of age were discharged from medical follow-up at this stage. The 'take-up' rate averaged 85-90 per cent. This is not particularly surprising, for given the doubt that surrounded the health status of a child admitted to the nursery the worry that mothers evidenced about this significant break in the relationship at such an early age was great. Thus, the motivation to turn up for follow-up was high, while the number discharged as 'normal' were also high. Indeed, 'normality' was such a feature of this clinic that the doctor once remarked somewhat surprised, 'There was quite a bit of pathology today'. Otherwise the clinic's clientele were 'boringly normal'.

The typical check

Clinics followed a typical format. To begin with parents were welcomed, children's identity established, and general questions asked about how the child had been, e.g. 'Are there any problems?'

From this the doctor moved on, briefly, to a sequence of standard test items such as cube handling, words, hearing, and sight, before a quick physical examination. Once completed, the doctor moved on to questioning the mother about worries that she mentioned during the previous phases or to worries that the mother was presumed to have about the child that remained unvoiced.

Thus, compared to the 'audience' role of the mother in the maternity rounds the mother had another identity to play. At ten months children had acquired a biography to which only the mother was privy in detail and usually they had a number of 'stories' they could tell based on their observation of the child over a period of time at home. Also, given the fact that 'serious' problems had existed in the past and potentially in the present as well, it was important to involve the mother to elicit these fears. For merely to discharge a child with a serious medical history is not the same as to indicate that all was now well. The child had to be *seen* to be well by the parents. Thus, parents were on the agenda, as well as the children.

One distinct advantage that the doctor had was the record and his knowledge of the likelihood of neonatal illness having implications for the current health of the child. Thus, the session was one where additional data was sought to confirm that the child was well enough to be discharged at this point. The unresolved issues were the parents' reactions to this discharge (and consequently parental worry) and whether any further follow-up would produce anything worth treating.

While the organizational reasons for mothers' attendance at the clinic were clear enough to the doctor, it was not at all clear to the parent. The only time the limits for clinic attendance were spelt out were on two occasions where parents attempted to use the clinic for treatment of chest infections and cradlecap, treating the clinic as if it were an opportunity for a 'consultation' and not a follow-up. Both were told firmly, 'We don't deal with *that* here'. Indeed, the opening question about 'problems' remained ambiguous — it was not clear what a correct answer would be. Most parents mentioned some fairly trivial childhood illness, coughs, colds, and so on, and left it at that. While parents knew their child was ill in the nursery it was never clear whether parents actually knew what had been wrong, indeed the reason for nursery treatment was only rarely alluded to at all. Consequently, most parents seemed to have little idea of what the follow-up was for, or what the doctor was looking for. Most had not got any immediate presenting problem (*that* lay in the past) and consequently had no definitely relevant medically oriented story that they could legitimately 'tell' on entry to the clinic, nor any clear idea of what such a story would look like.

Consequently, parents awaited the doctor's performance passively, responding to his questions until it became clearer that 'stories' were allowed about feeding difficulties, sleep problems, and so on in the context of the doctor's general concern with the child. Thus, putting the follow-up into a 'problem' formulation from the beginning created difficulties for the parents. As the medical services had recalled them, presumably for good reason, connected with past neonatal illness, the intrusion of a current 'problem' formulation produced hesitant, puzzled answers to what was obviously an unexpected question. Again, this is due to the nature of initiative medicine. It is clear in initiative medicine whose definition of problem has priority — the doctor's, for they have initiated the encounter to check on something specific. For the doctor to present an encounter generated in the 'initiative' mode as a 'receptive' one instead served to produce confused parents. Having been summoned for medically generated priorities and then to be asked, in effect, why they had come, was to introduce ambiguity and uncertainty as to what was going on, what was relevant and what was not, and *which* medical problem was being addressed, the 'past' one or the minor present one. The parents who took up the offer of this 'consultation' mode only found that their attempted 'consultations' were regarded as illegitimate by the doctor. They had no knowledge of the clinical agenda that was in practice concerned with a different kind of problem altogether, namely the parents' typification of the child.

There were occasions when the agenda did become more manifest. As noted earlier this was a clinic where teaching was also done. Scheduling of activities was complicated by the doctor's need to instruct any students present about normal and abnormal development. The doctors produced a clinical history of the child for the students but normally this was not done in the presence of the mother and child. Once, however, a nurse was rebuked for not allowing sufficient time for the doctor to talk to students before showing a mother and child into the clinic, truncating the teaching session abruptly.

Also, in running a busy clinic the doctor had limited time to demonstrate to students aspects of child development on each child. Instead each child was used to exhibit different interesting features. On two occasions in attempting to display the *absence* of some pathological feature the doctor suddenly became aware that he was raising new doubts and had to directly and emphatically tell parents that it was 'just teaching' and their child definitely did *not* show the feature he was talking to students about.

Normally though, teaching and clinical concerns were kept separate in time from screening. Teaching was done between patients.

The busy nature of the clinic also militated against any great involvement with the parent. The one exception was a doctor and her child, for whom students were banished from the room. The emphasis on speed meant that defaulters or latecomers were mildly rebuked unless their excuse was a 'good' one, e.g. a bomb scare at the local railway station.

Answers to questions about the competences of the ten-month-old child were easier for the mother to provide. By keeping the medical reason for the follow-up covert, the reasons for the doctor's questions also remained hidden, leaving them free to define relevance, what could be ignored and what was important. The doctor remained firmly in control of the session, switching topic or activity at will in order to conform to his medically generated clinical priorities. Thus, very pronounced switches in the doctor's interests were evident. Children would be quickly excluded from the encounter, distracted by a toy after being greeted, or described as if they had great interactional significance on entry to the clinic, for example, 'My, you *do* look well, don't you?'. The mother's follow-up comment on this remark would be quickly dismissed to move on to more important matters. In fact, the toy served a dual purpose, distracting the child as well as providing evidence of interest in surroundings, alertness, and normal dexterity. The result of this switching was to create ambiguity as to the precise focus of the encounter.

Worries

The initial 'problem'-oriented questions to the mother were carried forward into the examination, her 'minor' worries resolved by the doctor not finding anything wrong on examination. Thus a mother's suggestion that the child had bronchitis was dismissed after examination as 'Just a wee bit wheezy, nothing to worry about'. The developmental tests were also usually put into the form of question and answer. As the doctor performed tests with more or less success with more or less recalcitrant children the mother was used as a further check on what the doctor found, e.g. after hearing test (doctor to mother): 'You've no worries about his hearing, have you?' Mother replied. 'No'. Doctor said (watching child), 'No, he's turning [to sounds] fine'.

The main formulation of questions was, as we said in terms of 'worries' or 'problems' that the mother might have or have noticed. The 'worries' were never the doctor's worries, if he had them, or the past neonatal illness. Rather, the constant repetition of 'problems' or 'worries' was anchored firmly in the present and seemed designed to elicit anxieties the mother might have about the child rather than any 'worries' the doctor might have about the child. This constant prompting, of course, produced 'worries', but these had to be of the right kind. Snuffly noses, sore bottoms, colds and wheezes were normal enough in children and the production of these as 'worries' was irrelevant to the doctor's main concern. Such ailments were dismissed firmly and shortly as 'trivial', 'normal', or 'they are all like that at this age'. Such parental stories were dismissed in a number of other ways as well. Commonly the doctor would break into the middle of the mother's story, abruptly formulating the child for the mother in such a way as to foreclose all possible answers bar agreement.

For example, in one admittedly extreme case, the mother suddenly brought out a very complicated family history that was foreclosed by the doctor.

(D) 'From what you tell me he's doing fine. He's doing fine. He's well within the normal range.'

(M) Goes into a long story about her husband's brother who is mad, thinks he's from another planet and how he was going to be put away as 'You just canna talk to him', and she's worried baby will be like this. (D breaks in)

(D) 'Well, this sort of thing doesn't tend to be inherited, especially not from your husband's brother and as I said from all you've told me he's doing *very well*, well in the normal range. In fact his talking is rather *ahead* for his age *and* his walking.'

(M) 'Oh, *good*. I've been awfa worried.'

On the other occasions the story could be told at a time when it did not interfere with something else the doctor was doing. Thus, the doctor would typically ignore it and switch topics to something he was more interested in. Also, stories were curtailed by breaking in and stating their major theme, but not any subsidiary embellishments, as a conformatory finding. Or, more infrequently, the initial question might be asked again, indicating that the mother had not yet answered it correctly. Not surprisingly, as sessions wore on parents got more and more hesitant about what was required of them.

The continued probing for 'worries' usually revealed the 'correct' ones that mothers are presumed to have in the end. In fact, these 'worries' seemed to be the main concern of the encounter. As most of the children were normal, the doctor was dealing only with residual doubt about the child's normality; not clinical doubt, but parental doubt. Thus, the main item of attention seemed to be the mother and not the child and the whole tone of the encounter seemed designed to confer a normal childhood identity and to allay mothers' 'real' fears. Thus, the overt reason for recall became the mothers' worries and not the original clinical problem.

Once such worries were out in the open mothers were assured in a number of ways that the child's neonatal illness had no implications for their current status as normal child, and what is more, parents were overtly presented as competent to undertake the task of future surveillance of the child. Thus, presumed parent dependency on medical services was undermined by assurances that not only was the child normal but the mother was competent to take any further 'trivial' ailments to a GP rather than to treat them as indicative of some more sinister underlying health problem. While there may have been grounds for 'worry' before, to have 'worries' now was to be pathological about it. For mothers to cease to worry was to heal the child, for 'if you're happy, then I'm happy'. The child was not at issue. What was at issue was the mother's typification of the child.

Affirming normality

The clinic climate for normalizing and reassuring was created in a number of ways. To begin with, the questions and testing of the child were done in a manner that indicated they were not really problematic. Mothers' answers to questions about children's competences were not doubted, nor were they elaborately checked for internal consistency by overlapping and recapitulation as they were in receptive consultations.

Other tests, like seeing if children respond to their names in hearing tests, were typically fraught with difficulty, simply because of the many possible stimuli in the room; doctor, students, nurses, mother, and various noises off. Such tests had to be undertaken with caution. Thus, in one reported case when a child adamantly refused to turn to his name Robert, eventually the embarrassed mother cleared up the ambiguity by telling the doctor that the child was known by a nickname — 'Bubbles'.

Rather, the mother was treated as a reliable informant capable of reporting without any distortion on her child's abilities. The meaning of such questions was held to be self-evident when compared with questions about 'worries', as were the answers. Even when confronted by ambiguous or 'failed' test results, the ambiguity was resolved by reference to the mother. Issues about extent of vocabulary, meaning, and understanding words, adequate hearing responses, correct vision, and so on were treated as not problematic. If the child could or would not demonstrate on demand then the mother's word was taken for it. The child was never pushed. Excuses for the child were invariably honoured; for example:

> (D) 'Can he use a spoon?'
> (M) 'Well . . . I've never really tried him.'
> (D) 'Well, many don't at this age.'

Also, any failure to perform was explained away by the doctor often by reference to the setting and nature of the props, e.g.:

> (D) (Coaxing a child) 'Come on, don't let your Mummy down (smiles at M) . . . No ? . . . I think it's all the people here.'
> *or*
> (D) 'She's not very interested in that, is she? Never mind. It doesn't matter.' (Testing vision)

Such performances were assimilated to the character that all children possess, distractable, wilful, unpredictable, and so on. Children who refused to perform could easily be described as normal, e.g., 'She's a lively one, isn't she?', or 'He's very placid — is this an accident?' (smiles). (M) 'Oh, no — he's *good*'. Or 'You're bright today — into everything — you're interested in everything, aren't you?'

It was in this clinic that recourse to normal childhood was used most frequently to establish the child's normality. Thus, unpredictability, faddishness, boredom, and general incompetence were most frequently commented on to constitute the child as normal. Breaches of clinic order were sufficiently common to provide the doctor with plenty of evidence that the child was an ordinary child and to comment on such behaviour to the mother as normal.

During the examination the doctor continually gave off normalizing cues through the running commentary he gave on what he was doing. Thus, children were smiled at, greeted as bundles of joy, their antics and interventions laughed at, while at the same time the conversation with mother was interspersed with remarks to the child — 'You're good at that, aren't you — are you coming up? — hey!' and so on.

As we noted earlier, some worries were directly incorporated in the test and examination in such a way that the testing and examination refuted them. Thus, one mother who was adamant her child was not weight-bearing and seemed anxious about it, had her child placed in front of her by the doctor for part of the examination when he remarked, somewhat triumphantly, 'See — he *is* bearing weight on his legs — see . . . he is standing'. All the mother could do was agree.

Similarly, mothers in contact with other authorities sometimes used these to discredit the child's abilities. Thus, one mother quoted a health visitor and someone else as pronouncing the child 'A bit delayed'. The doctor retorted, 'They shouldn't have said that, it's not *that* certain', and then went on to display to the mother the child's normality on all the test and examination items. At other times the mother's 'problem' turned out to be trivial, but nevertheless existed. Thus, a mother's claim that the child suffered from 'terrible chests' that incapacitate the child. On examination the doctor admitted the child is 'wheezy' but nothing more. The mother's protestations of its seriousness was answered by a joke about her reliance on proprietary cough mixtures producing profits for drug companies but nothing else!

Other questions were answered in such a way as to render them innocuous. Thus, in response to a question about feeding difficulties, the doctor remarked, 'Mothers often ask me about this', rendering the problem a general one, a common one and therefore not a particularly troublesome one, certainly not dramatic, unexpected, or revelatory of some underlying problem.

Another means of providing a definitive typification of the child as normal was to invite the audience present to admire the child.

Where such an audience was partly medically expert such invocation carried a lot of weight, if only of numbers. Thus, when the doctor presented the child as normal to the mother with an invocation of an audience, all the mother could do was accept it, e.g.:

(D) 'Isn't she marvellous?' (To nurse)
(N) 'Yes, she is.'
(D) (To mother) 'You *must* be pleased with her?'
(M) 'Uh-huh.'

In other cases the doctor transformed the 'problems' into jokes. Thus, in one case the doctor was discharging he joked, 'You don't need to come here just for dandruff!' Also, children could be 'funny'. Thus, in one case the doctor mock-seriously told the nurse to subtract the weight of one block from the child's weight as the child was holding on to one of the clinic cubes at the time. Similarly, listening to one child's chest the doctor remarked, 'He sounds just like an old man who's been smoking twenty cigarettes a day', before agreeing the child was a bit wheezy.

As on the maternity round, such jokes are important, for how could such an amusing and delightful child be abnormal? Laughter can be cruel, yet to laugh on an occasion of serious concern would be to violate all kinds of rules about the proper, polite objects of humour. Handicapped or abnormal children are not legitimate targets of humour, particularly by 'caring' professions.

As well as the appeals to normal childhood so far mentioned, the doctor also used appeals to individual authority. The doctor used himself as an overt authority. This was rare. Definitive use of '*I* think she's perfectly normal' lays both individual and professional authority on the line. They were never directly challenged. In one case the doctor referred to the fact that 'Other doctors were concerned' but went on to say definitely, 'But *I* can see she's a normal little girl'. The same is true of the use of the word 'obvious', again an unusual term for doctors to use. It cropped up frequently in this clinic, e.g. 'She's obviously doing well' and 'It's obvious everything is all right so there's no reason to see him again'. Such self-evident normality cannot be challenged without the parent risking being typed as either dense or a pathological worrier.

Where the illness in the neonatal period was serious, discharge was presented as the final point in a modern medical miracle, as in one case:

(D) (To students) 'This baby was very ill at birth. She was nine weeks early and had severe hyaline membrane infection.

We had to put her on the ventilator. She was pretty ill in
every respect.' (Grins at C) 'You are lucky you weren't born
twenty years earlier, my girl.'
  (M) 'Otherwise you'd be dead!'
  (D) 'A triumph of modern medicine!'

The 'system' could also constitute a normalizing appeal. Thus, in
a couple of cases the nature of bureaucracy was appealed to explain
why the child was at the clinic at all. There were no medical
grounds but instead mindless bureaucratic necessity. This
particular appeal was reserved for another doctor's child and a
follow-up that had been summoned to attend from over a hundred
miles away by mistake. Thus, the routine follow-up was done but
prefaced by appeals to exterior bureaucratic necessity. Despite
this, the routine proceeded ineluctably.
  Despite the normality of most of the children seen and the
elaborate use of hyperbole and normalizing procedures to remove
parental worry some children (a minority) did turn out to have
something wrong with them. Interestingly, even here the children
were normalized. Thus, in one of the three cases, after being unable
to elicit any worries from the mother, the doctor announced that
the child's head was growing quickly and explained to the surprised
mother how this occurred. The child was admitted to hospital 'for
some tests' on the spot, 'to save you a journey in tomorrow
morning'. However, the child was pronounced 'doing fine in
himself' despite the revealed serious medical problem. Similarly,
the further recall of a child with a storage syndrome was done in
terms of some tests that might have to be done in the future, 'but
otherwise he's doing fine'. In both cases the essential normality of
the child was presented as intact despite an overt clinical problem.
In the third case, the doctor discharged the child, normalizing as
usual, but then said to students present that the child was slow and
backward. The justification for such a discharge was that the delay
was very marginal and further recall would only raise further
worries. In the fullness of time the mother would either raise it
with her GP, the school would pick it up, or the problem would
disappear altogether.
  Thus, the extravagant normalization noted in this clinic reflected
the doctor's concern to detach the patient from medical services, to
allay worries and to present the child as definitely normal. Such
reassurance was necessary as the doubt had at one point been
great.
  We argued before that initiative medicine of itself raises doubts
that it then has to resolve, whether by telling you that your chest

x-ray displays nothing noteworthy or by using demeanour and cues
'given' or 'given off' to create a sense of normality. We have seen
that typically screening implies standardization and the provision
of bench marks against which normality or abnormality can be
judged. In its strong form it can be educative and all-embracing in
its concerns and in its weak form a surreptitious check on progress.
As we noted in the Local Authority clinics the strong form was
eschewed largely due to the presumption of normality and the
marginal and weakly legitimated nature of that form of medicine.
But, the issue of 'normality' once raised must be addressed in some
fashion to resolve it. Typically in the Local Authority clinics a
friendly, concerned passivity; an assumed reciprocity of perspectives; a due deference to childhood and continual demedicalizing
worked together to defuse a potentially difficult situation. The
strong form of screening, a reformist version, was not attempted
or attained.

In the two hospital settings we noted other ways in which the
potential of screening for uncovering abnormality has handled; in
the maternity hospital by tight agenda control, limited involvement,
reassurance and talk to constitute normality and in the follow-up
clinic by continual normalizing and by rooting out and addressing
presumed worries that mothers might have that could lead to
dependency on medical services. In both, teaching cut across these,
creating some tensions solved either by invocation of the audience
as support or segregating clinical discussion from the actual
performance of work.

In both cases the normalizing proffered an identity of childhood
normality despite 'failure' through physical abnormality or
through non-performance of test items. Neither was presented as
serious. In both, the 'medicalness' of the occasion was undermined
by refusal to spell out the *reasons* for doubt and by continued
presentation of the screening as routine and not medically
problematic. As the parents' grounds for doubt increased as in the
special nursery follow-up clinic, then the widest range of
normalization was found.

As we said before, not only must children in such circumstances
be said to be 'normal' but they must also be treated as normal. Here
is the central paradox. If the child is normal (and most will be) the
considerable effort must be devoted to recreating that normality in
a context that puts the child in doubt, however temporary. Such
restorative work in such contexts then becomes a prime concern of
medical practice.

5

Receptive Medicine

The receptive form of medical encounter is the one most typically associated with the sick-role formulation. The person feels unwell, seeks expert advice on how to remedy this, and follows that advice because he wants to get better.

The hospital doctors and therapists we observed received clients whose dubious health status had already received prior validation by a GP or another hospital specialist. They received their 'trade' and controlled it in rather a different manner to those practising 'initiative' medicine.

The general medical clinics and special clinics studies were in a rather different position *vis-à-vis* their trade. They dealt with referrals from within the hospital as well as referrals from GPs outside. The initial referral might be made to a particular doctor or to the hospital in general. Thus, the job of primary sorting of patients fell on the booking clerks who booked cases into particular clinics if requested in the referral letter, returned 'old' cases to the clinic at which they were last seen, or routed cases to specialist clinics, if requested. Their activity caused considerable 'trouble' in clinics, as cases would often be, from the doctor's point of view, wrongly routed or wrongly booked.

In organizing the flow of work, doctors operated with assumptions about normal turn-up rates. Most clinics were 'over-booked' on the assumption that not all would turn up, an assumption that was the cause of much speculation about which particular clients could be safely relied on to default, thereby reducing the clinic trade to manageable proportions. Another way in which overall trade could be managed was by the doctor's own policy of recalls. Thus, one doctor had a large number of 'old' cases on his specialist clinic list because of his reluctance to discharge cases of suspected delay because he 'didn't trust the GPs to follow up'. In fact, this special clinic had been set up to take cases of mental and physical handicap out of the general clinics and to ensure follow-up that they were not getting before. Other doctors questioned the necessity for this, particularly if the doctors saw such cases as having little medical interest or little therapeutic potential.

The outcome of this scheduling was important, for it decided how long any particular patient got, and how 'slippage' on one case affected the rest of the clinic. Of course, it also affected the other activities of hospital doctors — to run clinics was only one of their jobs, they also had ward responsibilities, meetings to attend, research to do, and so on. Thus clinics running late potentially affected a number of their other activities so clinics had to be kept under strict control. To run late, or if every patient booked turned up, affected the amount of time that each patient could fairly be allocated. Thus, doctors not surprisingly insisted on the time allocation being kept to, on patients being ready and on call when required (a job the nurses did), and on the booking system working to their allocation of time within the clinic to enable them to keep ahead or on time. Time was subject to a running justice — the amount patients got depending on how well the doctor was coping with the current patient flow. One major booking disaster could (and did) throw the whole clinic off schedule to the irritation of doctors, patients, and nurses, and eventually led to complaints to the booking staff or to spectacular explosions of wrath — 'This clinic's gone to pot today', as one exasperated doctor shouted before summoning extra staff to help cope with the whole double booking that had occurred for his clinic as a result of his attempts to change his booking pattern for new and old patients.

Thus, doctors in differing degrees influenced the trade they got, either at one extreme being dependent on client initiatives, or at the other at the mercy of decisions made elsewhere in the medical system. Within this overall allocation of time and resources, the individual patient had little control over the amount of time they got. The bureaucratic management of clinic time owed more to the necessity of coping with demand and evening it out into a manageable queue than to patient-initiated requests. However, some cases, particularly the handicapped, were generally felt to require more time than 'normal', and were coped with by segregating such patients to a special clinic which saw far fewer patients per session than any of the others.

The general clinics were identified by the doctors who ran them as the core practice of paediatrics as a speciality. Despite further subspecialization within paediatrics, the doctors mentioned that this 'general' work was the main stuff of paediatrics, the diagnosis of childhood illness. These clinics consequently were also used for teaching medical students, so that an audience of students would usually be present as well as researchers. Their numbers were never as large as in the special nursery follow-up clinic (where numbers were often so great as to lead to ejection of some erstwhile students), but an audience of three or four could usually be counted on.

Consulting a specialist in such daunting surroundings presumably added to the parents' awe of the setting and militated against attempts at redefining the presenting problem once tentatively stated.

General clinics

All new cases were to begin with diagnostic problems. The object of the consultation was to sort out the 'ill' from the 'not ill' in the first instance. All cases came to such clinics with some prior medical doubt, usually the GP's opinion that a specialist consultation was necessary to adjudicate on the health status of the child. Such cases constituted the bulk of the cases seen in general outpatient clinics. The options open to the specialist were discharge, to hold pending tests, or diagnosis of illness and treatment. Such cases were exceptional problems for the GP, but constituted the normal trade for these general paediatric clinics. A large number of those seen at these clinics were discharged, after one consultation, as 'not ill', or if 'ill', as manageable by the GP. Much of this work was described by hospital doctors as 'trivial' or 'boring', being mainly concerned with the transient and non life-threatening illnesses to which most children are heir. Consequently, cases were approached with considerable scepticism, for the medical competence of the GP was also under inspection, a competence developed in dealing for the most part with non-serious illness and not in specialist practice of paediatrics.Thus the presumption was that most children presenting at these clinics would turn out to be well or suffering from transient illness.

In order to perform the task of sorting, the doctors employed a number of different procedures. Typically, to begin with, concern was shown over the status of the referral before the patient got into the clinic. The referral note was worked over in detail, it was 'read' to see if it gives any indication of the quality of the referral agent, to assess whether the information contained in it demonstrably led to the diagnosis tentatively proposed by the GP. It was here that the current state of knowledge about particular ailments was invoked to test whether the GP had got it right. Of equal importance was whether the GP had provided a description of the problem based on systematic observation, second-hand parental reporting, or whether the referral note showed evidence of the GP attempting to shed pressure put upon him by parents to refer the child. Thus, referral notes were routinely dissected to see what could be meant by vague terms such as 'late onset' or dubious diagnoses such as 'bronchiactus'.

A second typical procedure to establish the status of the referral was inspection of the existing hospital record, to construct a medical history of the child and in particular to see whether anything contained in the record could be seen to have a bearing on the current presenting problem as described by the GP.

Thus, before the patient was seen, the specialist had already constructed a probabilistic model of the likelihood of the illness, its seriousness, its thematic relationship to the child's previous medical biography as well as the status of the child in relation to the normal trade of the clinic, as well as the reliability of the GP.

A third typical procedure was to request a statement from the parent accompanying the child as to what the problem was. Hence our term 'receptive' to describe the stance of the doctor to the client. In initiative medicine this 'problem' formulation was not used, except in the special nursery follow-up clinic. The problem instead was constructed in advance by the doctor. This invitation to the parent to describe the 'problem' was done in the most general manner and constituted an invitation to tell a *story* about the child's presenting problem. However, once this had been given, it was re-worked by the specialist according to his priorities. Thus, 'stories' had their uses as opening statements of how the parent interpreted the child's health status and what they had been told by the GP, but for diagnostic work they had to be reordered in a form that allowed the specialist to fit described events to likley illness patterns. Consequently, the parents' story was broken down into elements that had medical relevance and that were not contaminated by parents' own diagnoses. No interpretation was allowed, but questions were asked that required answers in terms of 'natural' descriptions of sequences of events in the presumed illness. Attempts at interpretation were resisted. For example, in describing a child's chestiness, one parent referred to it as 'hay fever'. The specialist responded by asking, 'What do you mean "hay fever"?' in order to obtain more detailed descriptions of symptoms (see Byrne and Long 1976).

One important feature of this procedure was its orientation to the present rather than the past. The description required was of the presenting problem only and questions were directed at this alone in any detail. What was being sorted was 'evidence' for there being a problem *at all*, rather than an investigation into the status of the child in general. The child's state was until proved otherwise normal, but possibly ill, and it was to that possible illness that questioning was directed, not at the status of the child in general.

Another purpose was served by this detailed questioning of the parent, that of matching the 'story' of the parent to the medically relevant answers to questions and to the 'story' of the illness as presented by the GP. The correspondence of the accounts was of considerable importance in establishing the credibility of the supposed illness, particularly if the 'story' held up during questioning without yielding any discrepancies.

The fourth typical procedure was to take a medical history. Typically, this was brief as it was taken for granted that anything out of the ordinary would be in the record already. Again, the attenuated history was mainly directed at previous childhood illnesses and not centrally at the developmental status of the child. This was then followed by a brief examination, again mainly directed at the current physical state of the child.

The final procedure was a definitive statement about the health status of the child, usually a rejection of any serious problem and a confirmation that it was a transient, non-threatening condition that would either pass in time or required minimal treatment that could be carried out by the GP. This summary also incorporated reassurance about any features that the parent has said worried them about the child earlier in the consultation, though the emphasis placed on the *current* problem by the doctor ensured that few of these were, in fact, raised at all.

These, then, were the typical procedures the doctors used in order to reach a disposal decision within the ten to fifteen minutes allocated to each case on the clinic list.

Ideally, as noted earlier, for the clinic to operate smoothly it required prior medical information, a parent prepared to cede the right to diagnosis to the specialist with the implied right for the specialist to question at will, and the parent to present good raw data on which the doctor could effect a diagnosis. To accomplish this in the allotted time required the parent to cede criteria of relevance fully to the doctor, giving appropriate answers to doctors' questions without demanding the demonstration of the thematic unity of such questioning and to accept the summary definitive statement at the end without question. Where this relationship was maintained, an orderly clinic ensued. However, there also were a number of ways in which the clinic order could be breached with consequent remedial problems for the doctor. The problems rarely emanated from the child, who was relegated to a walk-on role in the main drama that took place between doctor and parent. Rather, the problems surrounded cases which in various ways breached implicit rules concerning the rationale for the clinic and the proper identities of the participants in it, namely the status of the referral the credibility of the evidence, the parent, and where the parents misdefined the nature of the clinic, all of which impeded the task of diagnosis.

Clinic order

Some cases came to the clinic without any indication of why they were referred, lacking either a referral letter or obvious reason for re-referral from another clinic. Nevertheless, appearance of cases on the clinic list was assumed to be medically warranted. The problem was just why they were there. In such cases where there was no stated presenting problem it was unclear what is expected of the doctor by the referrer or referred, what problem he should address himself to and no 'independent' check on what might be presented as 'the problem' by the parent in the clinic. Such cases provided no independent information from which the questioning can start; nor did it necessarily mean that the story told by the parents can be taken as the 'real' reason for attendance. Such cases caused much speculation and reference to the medical record to see if that provided any clear indications of what the problem might be.

Responses to this ambiguity were usually constructed out of the last thing in the medical record, so that the doctor would begin the consultation as if the last thing noted in the record constituted the current problem until the parent volunteered a reason for attendance. Only then would the new problem be addressed. Should this fail, doctors were eventually forced to ask why the parent had turned up, an embarrassing admission of ignorance that was potentially damaging to the status of the doctor or the administration of the hospital. Thus, such cases would typically begin with a run-through of the previous problem and its current status until the reason for attendance and the referrer's status became self-evident through parents initiating topics of conversation. Once this was available, then the doctor could reimpose his normal diagnostic routines to manage the clinic.

A similar ambiguity surrounded a referral letter which asked for 'a check' for two young girls. Again the ambiguity was resolved by asking very general questions until sufficient parental 'worries' had been voiced, and these were taken as the presenting problem. Only much later did it emerge that the 'check' was for the general health of the children before they returned to the tropical island where their parents worked. At this point, problems in child development in tropical climates became the 'problem' that was addressed systematically. Such cases were also ambiguous because they presented no obvious illness for diagnosis. Given the general orientation of the clinic to rule out the presence of illness, it was unusual for the doctor to be asked positively to confirm existing health, an activity unusual to such a clinic.

Other cases turned up at the clinic through administrative error. Thus, some ward discharges appeared on clinic lists by mistake. Nothing could be served by such attendances given the primary concern of diagnosis and such cases received short shrift and an apology for their unnecessary and embarrassing presence.

Another set of problems surrounded the credibility of the evidence available to use as a basis for diagnosis, and the credibility of the parent. This was particularly important where the sufferers themselves could not be used to produce clear and precise descriptions of symptoms. A four-month-old baby presented as being suspected of suffering from epileptic attacks presented little data for interpretation in an out-patient clinic, particularly as the GP offered no direct observations and the parents were unable to present sufficient data to confirm a possible diagnosis. The only alternative in such cases was in-patient observation, deferment of tests, or setting up repeat appointments to confirm or refute the diagnosis. Such problems were not easily resolvable through normal out-patient clinic attendances. Nor were cases where the parents' story and the GP's story seriously diverged. Here the strategy became one of testing the credibility of the parents' story and assessing which of the two possible 'problems' was the one to be addressed.

Where the story from the parent was confused or ambiguous and at odds with the version provided by the GP the credibility of the parents' story was always assessed by close and detailed questioning, going back over the story several times to test whether it was internally consistent and using the examination and observation of the child to adjudicate on whose version was correct. Such 'puzzles' usually required further medical tests to establish the credibility of one or other of the accounts of the problem. As well as repetition and consistency, the doctor used other methods of assessing the story, by suggestion and comparison in an attempt to produce better descriptive terms, e.g. 'Is it *like* asthma, then?', or the use of check questions to test the consistency of the story of illness against other aspects of the child's behaviour. Thus, doctors routinely checked whether, for example, a child who claimed to be prostrated and debilitated by recurrent headaches also went out playing in the street and was otherwise active or whether a child with perpetual chest trouble from which 'he's never clear' was out playing in the school holidays long enough to acquire a suntan. A similar purpose was served by suggesting that the description of illness is over-emphasized in comparison to the child's relative normality. Thus, parents responded to the question, 'Do you normally think of him as a healthy boy?' by putting the severity of the illness in a proper perspective of an illness *episode* interrupting the otherwise normal status of the child rather than as some disabling and life-threatening chronic condition.

The following extract from a consultation with a four-year-old boy with possible febrile convulsions illustrates most of the features we have described so far:

- (D) 'Hello Mrs. Smith. Do sit down. This is William, is it?'
- (M) 'Yes.' (sits)
- (D) 'Hello William, do you want to look at this car while I'm talking to your Mother?'
- (C) 'Yes.' (goes and plays in corner)
- (D) 'And William's now four?'
- (M) 'Yes, four last April.'
- (D) 'And he has fits on occasions, your doctor says? He's been having them since December?'
- (M) 'The first was in December.'
- (D) 'Could you tell what happened then?'
- (M) 'No, not really.'
- (D) 'No, I see ...'
- (M) 'My wee girl was in here. I came in and collected her and when I got home, my mother was holding him. He was unconscious and he was a bit sick and jerky. She was very worried about it?'
- (D) 'And what happened then?'
- (M) Elaborates on story.
- (D) Becomes more directive, asking what the GP said and saw.
- (M) 'He said he had a temperature each of the three times.'
- (D) 'Was there any reason for this?'
- (M) 'No, not really. It was just like a cold ...'
- (D) 'How long was he ill for altogether in December?'
- (M) 'Well, he was all right at the end of the day.'
- (D) 'But there wasn't any evidence *before* that he had a cold at this time?'

Doctor then asks more directive questions about the second and third attack, did he bite his tongue did he pass urine, how long did it last, etc. any fever, duration (a second time).

A further set of problems revolved around the taken-for-granted rules about how such diagnostic sessions should take place. Thus, on one occasion, a consultant had to spell out the rules to follow to get to see a consultant to a disbelieving American mother who had somehow appeared on the clinic list with a problem that 'should' properly have been treated by a GP. This particular consultation was conducted in a brusque and irritated manner; the mother had turned up without the necessary prior medical warrant. On another occasion when a couple attempted to pay the consultant on the spot for the consultation, the consultant, amused, spelt out the financial basis of the NHS; the consultation was legitimate as it had been set up by a GP. These gross mistakes over how the clinic operated were very rare. Other, still rare, occasions for misdefinition of the task and clinic did occur over issues of relevance and the unit of consultation.

To begin with relevance rules, given that the clinic existed to deal with presented medical problems, some interpreted the medical remit in a wider fashion than did the doctor.Thus, as the doctor typically decided what was relevant and what was not, failure to take up the cues lead to a brusque redefinition of the parents' attention within the clinic and a statement on the limits of the consultants' interest in the child. Thus, parents had considerable leeway in initially stating the problem as they see it, but then were expected to cede to the doctor the right to direct his questions to 'relevant' issues and having done so follow the cues implicit in such questioning by confining themselves to answers to remarks which have a direct relevance to the question. This pattern conformed closely to the doctor-centred model described in Byrne and Long (1976).

The few parents who did not do this caused obvious irritation to the doctor. A grandmother who used a consultation over her grandchild's incontinence to launch an attack on the morality of the mother and on the maternity and surgical services was studiously ignored until she had finished. The next statement from the doctor referred back to an earlier question of admitting the child to hospital. Refusal to take up questions of obvious importance to the parent indicates their irrelevance and inappropriateness. Such cases were rare and normally parents did not seek to direct the doctor's attention to features of the case except those he himself chose to select. Only in one case did parents in fact challenge the doctor's diagnosis. As described earlier, the typical consultation ended with a summary and definitive statement by the doctor of the child's health status. In face of this expert pronouncement that there was no problem, or only a minor one, most parents sat (gratefully it appeared) and accepted the final diagnosis without question. However, one couple used the final statement as the occasion to challenge the doctor's diagnosis by stating new evidence which typified the child as 'out of control' and 'hyperactive'. The doctor took this as a new presenting problem and worked through a series of questions that cast doubt on the credibility of this formulation, using the child's silence and immobility in the clinic as confirmatory evidence for his diagnosis of the child as perfectly normal and healthy. However, the parents then attempted to discredit the child further by suggesting that the child had something seriously wrong with it that would interfere with the child's schooling. After reiterating the 'findings' that nothing was wrong with the child, by assimilating the parents' worries to a picture of a normal childhood development, referring to his expertise, by countering the evidence presented by parents with counter-evidence of normality, the parents stated that the child was an 'educational' problem. At this point, the doctor overtly drew the lines of medical involvement, stating that the problem, if it existed, should properly be dealt with by the educational authorities and not him, and that future questions about the child's education should be directed at the school or school medical service. This was done in a manner which brooked no argument, firmly stated the limits of medical relevance, and indicated that no more could be expected of him. At this point the consultation ended. Such diagnostic challenges were rare indeed and order in these clinics was maintained intact without serious breakdowns.

Where the normal clinic techniques failed to produce a definite outcome, a firm diagnosis, further procedures were invoked that would remove the ambiguity. The child could be recalled to check on subsequent progress, or admitted to hospital, but this had certain disadvantages in that it raised the level of worry that the parents displayed. The value of such recalls was matched against their likely impact on the parents. In such cases, the medical urgency of the case was weighted against the level of anxiety displayed by the parent in the clinic as a basis for recall. Another option was to arrange more specific tests to rule out the possibility of serious illness, e.g. brain tumours. However, the emotionally charged possibility of this option was usually played down in its significance. Such tests were presented as 'a check' or 'routine' events just 'to make sure' that nothing is wrong. Rarely were they presented in a manner that indicated that they might yield serious results. Indeed, their relative insignificance was stressed by one doctor who routinely told parents that they were not to attend again and would be informed of the test results by their GP. Thus, tests were presented as exercises in negative diagnosis — merely to confirm for the doctor that the child was not suffering from some illness.

In all the cases seen in general clinics, the items for discussion were supplied from an expert medical corpus of knowledge. Such consultations were exercises in distinguishing the 'ill' from the 'not ill'. The clinic, therefore, had a narrow remit and dealt with presenting medical problems or specific illness episodes. In such circumstances issues of parental responsibility, children's normality, and family circumstances in general were not relevant topics for investigation. Doctors might speculate in private about peculiarities in family dynamics, problems of living in particularly rough areas of the city, and parental competence, but did not incorporate these into the encounter with parents in any overt manner. The encounter was maintained as strictly medical. The large majority of cases were discharged or held pending the outcome of tests whose outcome was not in any serious doubt. Only three of the cases seen were diagnosed as requiring further medical attention, two with queries about delay, the third a case requiring monitoring of new drugs for abdominal migraine. The rest were discharged, their illness 'episodes' in no way questioning or impairing their essential normality.

Such consultations conform most closely to the traditional model of the doctor-patient encounter, the parent coming with a problem which 'needs' expert adjudication on the status of that problem. Such a presentation surrenders the right to the doctor to construct an agenda to reach a diagnosis and a disposal and renders the patient and parent passive in face of the diagnostic task performed in the clinic setting. In fact, the term 'consultation' correctly conveys the form of the encounter, client-initiated to seek medically expert information. Throughout these clinics there was a marked absence of marvelling at children. We noted they had walk-on roles, summoned for examination but otherwise ignored. They were not involved, but instead questioning was directed to the parents. This was important, for these features served to place the child in the category 'possibly ill' and that illness was of a transient kind that raised no questions about whether it could threaten the 'normal' identity of the child. All children are 'ill' from time to time, but such illnesses do not have status-threatening implications. Medical involvement in such cases was narrow and specific in its focus on the presenting problem, conforming closely to what McKeown calls the 'engineering model' of medical practice (McKeown 1976). The doctors used a corpus of knowledge concerned with human beings as biological systems to warrant treatment or exclusion from the category 'ill'. The main impediment to this accomplishment was that GPs and parents (particularly fathers) were more or less unreliable reporters of symptoms, and their stories had to be ransacked to establish their reliability and the parents' veracity. However, this form is limited to the one-off diagnostic encounter. In other forms of medical work the term 'consultation' does not convey the different quality of the interaction and does not adequately describe the relationship between doctor and parent. We call this mode of interaction 'medical maintenance.'

Medical maintenance

As noted in the previous section, some cases were held over on recall after diagnosis of a potential illness and for confirmation of the diagnosis by various tests, so, another type of attender regularly turned up at general paediatric clinics. There were 'old' cases, often with voluminous records, who were kept under review for the medical maintenance of a diagnosed pathological condition. Such cases were deemed to require regular routine follow-up and monitoring of their medical progress. They fitted easily within the constraints of the general clinic, requiring little medical servicing beyond a brief check that all was well.

The procedures for accomplishing the servicing fitted easily within the clinics' time limits of ten to fifteen minutes per case, particularly as the main task to be performed was that of 'checking', a task facilitated by the assumption that parents were aware of the diagnosis and experienced in the forms of treatment available. Thus, such cases proceeded from an assumed problem which no longer had to be directly addressed as diagnosis had been achieved. The main content of the interaction consisted of the doctor checking on the effects of treatment and the contribution of current medical endeavour to the amelioration of the old problem. This involved asking about the effects of the treatment regime, for example whether current dosages of drugs were containing epileptic seizures. Such questions assumed a parent competent to report any significant changes in the child's health and such questions did not have the interrogative quality which rendered the parent a passive provider of raw symptomatology. A further set of 'checks' were made to ensure that there were no *new* problems either produced by the treatment or manifesting themselves as indicators of other underlying pathology.

As well as these checks on the therapeutic efficacy of current treatment, the scope of questioning was routinely widened to enquire how the parents were managing the treatment regime at home and whether this management created any problems either for them or for the child. The final item that was invariably addressed was a reminder of the importance of following the treatment regime and reinforcing the value of such compliance. Parents were praised for their management skills, particularly where parental efforts could be demonstrably tied in with the child's medical progress, for, of course, all parents wanted their children to improve. What was required was the motivation and information to enable them to do so and to present their child at the next clinic with a further improvement. The atmosphere created by 'checking' was one of continual progress, of well — motivated parents working as part of a team to improve the health of the child. Such occasions then were friendly affairs, children admired and treated as valuable persons coming along well under the joint coaching of the doctor and parent.

In such circumstances, the parents were progressively becoming 'wiser' than parents presenting their child for initial diagnosis. Also, to maintain the parents' motivation to follow medication rules or avoid hazardous situations that might cause a child to come into danger, e.g. an epileptic boy riding a tricycle near a main road or swimming unsupervised, doctors routinely asked for and expect questions from the parents. The production of such questions reinforced doctors' conceptions of the parents' competence and they readily gave detailed explanations of aetiology, current status, and likely prognosis. Thus, the longer the parent attended, the more familiar the doctor became with the parent and child and the more the parent acquired medical information and knowledge of the clinic agenda and the doctor. As a result conversational civilities were more elaborate than were found in the consultation sessions.

Despite the easy relationship between doctor and parent, there were a number of points of tension in the interaction. These surrounded the typification of the child and the ambiguity induced by the requirement that the child be followed up at three- or six-monthly intervals, for 'checking' was not the same as 'discharged well' and indicates there was a medical problem still to be resolved.

One of the problems that doctors continually confronted was the management of the ambiguity of the child's health status. Such review cases can be and were sometimes seen by parents as evidence that their child was not normal but handicapped in such a way that the illness was a master status trait that incapacitated their child from entering into a normal round of childhood activities, such as playing, mixing with other children, going to school, or engaging physically active pursuits outside the home and requiring continuous parental supervision. Consequently, doctors took great pains to minimize any threatening aspect of illness and to stress the relative normality of such illnesses as epilepsy, migraines, laryngeal abnormalities, and galactazemia. For example, in the following extract the doctor is stressing the manageability of a chronic condition, emphasizing that it should not be seen as swamping other identities. (The child has a congenital laryngeal abnormality.) The child is currently in contact with a number of specialists.

> (D) 'If you are to see Mr X in February, then I think you'd better make an appointment for this clinic in April. I'd like to keep seeing her regularly. Are there any other issues?'
> (M) 'No, it's just colds and sicknesses.'
> (D) 'Yes it is a problem.'
> (M) 'Is it OK to have her in crowds? I mean, there's this party coming up, I was wondering if she could go to that?'
> (D) 'Well — yes — you can't keep her away. I think the *only* way to do it is to treat her like any other child. You've got to wait to see Mr X but you can't keep her away from parties and things.'

Though the illnesses may be chronic, they were repeatedly presented as non-stigmatic, so that the abnormality should in no way be seen as impairing the child's normality in all other respects. Instead, their manageability was stressed and the problem presented as in no way interfering with normal living. Indeed, with some it was possible to stress that they would eventually clear up altogether in the fullness of time e.g. urine infections. Others, while 'life sentences', were emphatically presented as not life-threatening once the parents had established routine management procedures. Parents were invited to voice their worries, to elaborate how they saw the child developing. Once voiced, attention was given to them with medically backed and categorical statements that their fears were misplaced or unwarranted. In clinics, the children would be treated as normal by the doctor, asked about enjoyed games, friends, in such a manner as to indicate that they were to be treated for practical purposes as normal children who just happened to have a minor medical problem.

Given that the day-to-day management of the child devolved onto the parent, a precondition for easily managed clinic 'checking' was that the parent had a routine established that they could report on, and sufficient information to show that its imposition had both point and purpose. Thus, for maintenance cases an educative task had to be performed. However, neither bald orders nor simple instruction could be relied on to produce compliance as parental

motivation had to be maintained as well as a willingness to co-
operate with the doctor. Consequently, domestic routines were
established in seminar-like sessions with the parents questioning
doctors and getting both practical and theoretical information, but
also with the doctor having the opportunity to stress the necessity
of the routines, their medical basis, and their practical importance.

For example, in the following extract the doctor is discussing
with parents the management of a child reaching school age with a
chronic kidney disorder. After discussing the child's weight the
doctor says:

(D) 'Well his weight is not all that bad for a child of his age.'
(M) 'Oh well, that's all right then.'
(D) 'But it's not really enough for his height of course it may
be his treatment or his illness. How much is he on?'
(M) 'He's on twenty-eight a week.'
(D) 'And that's been for a year has it?'
(M) 'Uh-huh, a year past.'
(D) 'Has had no illness in the past six months?'
(M) 'A cold'
(F) 'A summer cold.'
(D) 'You were on it (drug) four times a day weren't you?'
(M) 'Yes.'
(D) 'Do you still test his urine?'
(M) 'Yes, every week.'
(D) 'And it's still clear?'
(M) 'Yes.'
(D) 'Well, he'll need to carry on treatment for another year.
But I think we can reduce the dosage. If the urine is clear,
well, just cut it down to two times a day. If the albumen
comes back then put it up again. It will help him grow.'
(M and F then discuss whether child should have a bangle or
card detailing his condition for use at school in emergency.

This willingness to answer questions, and indeed, to invite them,
solved other important problems. As the parents' typification of the
child was constantly at risk of drifting into the handicapped
category, the doctor's demonstrable openness to question served
also to indicate that nothing was being hidden. Thus, parents could
be reassured that no dreadful prognoses were being hidden by the
doctor and that he was trustworthy. This problem was particularly
acute each time treatment or review was changed, or further tests
called for. The results of such tests were always given and parents
invited to ask questions which in effect tested the doctor's
trustworthiness. In one question-and-answer session, the mother

was asked to write out her questions for her next clinic attendance. The doctor had reassured the mother that the child had a chronic but not life-threatening illness. The mother returned to ask how old was the oldest child with this condition (not whether it was fatal), which produced an open debate amongst the doctors and dietician present about the oldest child they knew. They finally had to admit that they did not know but they would try to find out.

Willingness to give information also helped solve another problem, that of defaulting. If the doctor wished to follow up a case, he could normally rely on parental obligations to look to the welfare of their children to keep them attending. Nevertheless, some parents did default, despite demonstrations of willingness to answer questions and give practical advice and also praise. How were defaulters treated? While from the doctor's point of view there would seem to be grounds for indicating that parents were falling down on their moral responsibilities, to do so would have been to turn the clinic into a moralistic battleground with the likelihood of deterring the parent from braving the doctor's wrath in future. Instead, elaborate courtesy was displayed, gratitude for turning up despite presumed difficult circumstances at home or in organizing the family for a clinic attendance.

In one case where the family came from a known 'bad area' and where there was a history of defaulting throughout other hospital clinics, the mother was treated with elaborate courtesy when she did turn up, the 'accounts' she offered unrequested for non-attendance were honoured as perfectly reasonable, and the mother allowed to blame the hospital's appointment system for her failing to attend. Though judged to be untrue, the blame was accepted with sympathy at the effects of bureaucratic muddles in the hospital appointments system. The child's defaulting at posture classes in the hospital was accepted as reasonable when the mother explained that the child did not like attending along with 'the wee kids'. The same courtesy was shown to an itinerant tinker family on one of their infrequent attendances, despite the fact that on at least one occasion they had to be tracked down by the police in order to ensure medicine was being taken. Such a case as this was a source of wry amusement rather than moral censure.

Clinics, however, had their failures and these created problems, albeit of different severity, though of course, from the parents' point of view even 'minor' medical failures can loom large in their implications for the family. Thus, in some cases or review for some years, defeat had to be admitted once the medical recipes had all been tried in turn and failed. Thus, in one intractable case of encopresis and another of incontinence, specialist attention failed to yield any demonstrable improvement. In both cases, the burden of management was put firmly back into the families' province with one doctor saying that he hoped it would clear up 'in time' of its own accord, and another doctor to the other mother, 'Well, you're the doctor now, I'm afraid'. Where such 'burdens' could be maintained by judicious family management of laxatives, 'soiling' was a problem for which medicine had little or nothing to offer. However, in another case the temporary collapse of the family of an eneuretic child was deemed sufficient grounds for a hospital admission. After all, distant relatives could not be expected to undertake the job of managing and concealing from public a doubly spoiled identity.

Other failures were more serious, particularly if they were out in the open. Thus, a child on review for some years had not yet been diagnosed, a failure compounded by the parents having been told at an earlier point in time to prepare themselves for the child's imminent death, a threat that failed to materialize. This left the doctor very embarrassed, faced with parents who overtly doubted his credibility and the efficacy of medicine in general. Checking sessions with the parents were not anticipated with joy, but rather with gloom only relieved by the parents being 'in the circumstances very understanding'. These parents were received with elaborate courtesy and assurances that the doctors were doing their very best and still working hard to come up with a diagnosis. In this case 'checking' was done as a holding operation until a definite diagnosis could be reached.

So far, we have only considered those cases where the diagnosis is out in the open and available to the parents. There is another kind of case in which the overt activity was 'checking' but the deeper agenda was oriented to a problem other than that which was overtly being 'checked'. Typical cases in this category were ones where the presenting problem at which diagnosis has been directed had been superseded by the doctor's discovery or suspicion that another more serious problem existed. Thus, a tension existed between what was overtly 'checked' and what was actually 'checked', a tension produced by the inability of the doctor to present the 'checking' as indicating settled and shared diagnosis, progress, and a corresponding willingness to answer questions and provide information, all the normal procedures used to maintain motivation for attendance. Such cases then were in a medically ambiguous category that was potentially threatening in its implications for the future status of the child.

The doctors' rationale for maintaining this ambiguity was either that there was sufficient clinical uncertainty about diagnosis and prognosis for there to be good grounds for waiting before committing their expertise to one definitive diagnosis and prognosis. Another reason that co-existed with it was that in such cases it was in the interests of all concerned that parents should gradually come to terms with the new problem as it mainfested itself. 'Forcing' the status passage on unprepared parents was held to cause parents to undergo a more stressful experience than gradual realization of the new problem engendered. Further, given that such bad news had considerable implications for domestic organization, the effects of forced status were unpredictable. Consequently, time also provided a basis for typing the parent as one likely to handle sensibly or emotionally the bad news, should it ever have to be told.

Thus, while the overt activity was one of checking, the recall that checking implies allowed the doctor time to type the parents. On the other hand, the use of 'checking' brought with it a number of problems.

To begin with, the use of 'checking' made it difficult to prepare parents for worse to come. As 'checking' of necessity had to be orientated to something that needs 'checking', this was almost invariably the original presenting problem. Thus, doctors became trapped by orienting their interest to the overt problem and not to the planting of doubts that the presenting problem may not have been the 'real' one, simply because the possibility of a grave medical condition was never directly addressed. While for the doctor such 'checking' might have revealed as yet unresolved problems, it could have been read as merely indicating that the overt and not very serious problem had not yet been resolved by the parents. Parents, as yet, had no evidence to the contrary available to them. Qualified statements that all was not well could be, and were assimilated by the parents to a formulation of the child as not yet clear of the original illness episode which precipitated the referral.

Similarly, recalls were assimilated in the same way and not taken as indicative of a new problem, simply because they were presented as necessary for very vague reasons 'just to check how she's going on' or in terms of the original problem, 'I'll see him again in three months to see how the attacks are going on'. A suspicion of delay was covered by focusing on, for example, epiphenomenal epileptic attacks and not the delay itself. The planting of doubt through the absence of the normalizing cues and ambiguous recall reasons was rendered counter-productive where the presented reason for continued attendance was, for example, epileptic attacks and not the more threatening issue of delayed development.

Also typing the parents as competent to handle the bad news was hindered by parents' orientation to the presenting problem and not to the more threatening hidden prognosis of delay or handicap. Doctors had to rely on how parents appeared in clinics to provide clues as to what kind of parent they are. 'Checking' did not sufficiently widen the content of the agenda to encompass what parents are 'really' thinking, for what they are 'really' thinking about seemed to be the presenting problem and not the doctor's hidden suspicions. Thus, attempts to get the parents to talk about their views of the child's progress did not usually reveal very much, for 'progress' was taken to refer to the overt problem and not the 'real' one.

If the content of the checking had been the illness episode, then it was difficult to move from this to, for example, handicap, if only because the main topic of conversation had been and continued to be some specific illness episode that was unconnected with the doctor's main worry. Thus, qualified statements about the child being 'a bit behind' did not seem particularly threatening if epilepsy was being treated as the main issue. Not surprisingly, parents were able to resist these kinds of 'plants', if only because they were minor in relation to their professed main concern, the overt problem. The doctor, uncertain of diagnosis, prognosis, and parental acceptance was unable definitively to pronounce that the child was irreparably delayed or handicapped at that point, so such parental refutations were normally left to stand unchallenged.

The doctor's suspicions could be resolved, but not easily in the diagnostic clinic context. For suspicions of delay to be confirmed required time, and also systematic investigation and comparison of children's progress over a long period of time. Such a procedure implies a very different medical task, one that cannot be easily accomplished in the ten minutes allotted to the case. Should it turn out that the child was handicapped, then further issues of management were raised which again could not easily be settled in a ten-minute consultation.

In fact, the cases that fitted most uneasily into the general clinic format were cases of diagnosed physical and mental handicap. The doctors felt that parents got very little out of a rushed ten-minute session compared with the amount of organization and disruption that such attendance entailed, for the mother in particular. A check on current organizational arrangements for handling the child, any current health problems, or any counselling or advice could rarely be achieved in the ten minutes allotted to such cases in the general clinics. If medicine was ineffectual in such cases, then its ineffectiveness was heightened by the way in which serious issues were handled in an abbreviated manner. It was for this reason that a special clinic was established to handle such cases. Also, such cases breached the more dominant commitment of doctors to 'acute', 'technical' medicine. The requirements of handicap cases were deemed to require a very different stance and an imposed different type of doctor style more oriented to 'caring', 'understanding', and 'painstaking', rather than 'curing'.

Instead, such cases required a different clinic with different priorities and agenda. However, premature referral can itself create worries that may be unfounded. Doctors were trapped in a dilemma; should they refer all such cases immediately and accept the unnecessary distress that this would cause some parents, or 'hold' the case until the parents recognized the need for further medical work? In the mean time, ambiguity had to be tolerated.

This was partially resolved by systematically seeking to elongate the time-span beyond the normal illness episode. Terms such as 'We'll have to wait and see' were routinely used to stress the emergent nature of the problem, though again closely tied to the presenting problem. Examinations are delayed, 'We won't do anything now, we'll wait until he's older so we can see properly how he is going' because 'It's too early to say yet, one way or the other'. Thus, time became a continually omnipresent theme, justifying recalls and indicating that parents should abandon their expectations of an early solution, but instead wait for 'things to unfold', because 'we cannot rush things'.

Thus, by elongation of time, initially around the presenting problem, a different time perspective for the assessment of delay or handicap was indirectly imparted. Within such a longer time-span, of course, the parents (it was hoped) would also come to recognize that other problems exist. It was at this point that re-referral for specialist investigation was done. Meanwhile, parental assumptions of the normality of the child would remain unvalidated when expressed in the clinic, although the presenting problem would still be the rationale for recall. Hopefully, parents would gradually notice a lack of improvement, begin to wonder about the health status of their child, begin to check on the child's competences by comparing the child with others until they were ready to voice their doubts about the child in the clinc. In such cases, the re-referral then became an obvious solution to the parents' recognition of the new problem once it was voiced in the clinic; the doctor could agree with parental doubts and seek a resolution of them through referral. Where no such 'adjustment' took place, then the issue would eventually be forced despite its unpleasant repercussions and shock. By then, of course, the doctor felt both on safe ground to present such bad news and, moreover, under an obligation to bring it out into the open by his referring the child because 'He seems behind and I'd like another doctor who has more time to go into this further to see him. I'll arrange an appointment'. Such forcing was not always successful in changing the way in which parents viewed their children. As we shall see in a later section, even the gloomiest pronouncements could be and were ransacked by parents for hopeful implications, and for every defect a doctor found, it was often possible for the parents to produce counter-evidence that all was well. But these definitional battles took place at a later stage.

So far the clinics we have been describing conform to the normal model of the client-initiated encounter, though all these cases are ones which have received some validation by a GP in referring them for specialist attention. Already, though, we notice that there is some difference in the medical task and the relationship between doctor and parent. The diagnostic sessions were characterized by the parent ceding the right to the doctor to structure the consultation in order to achieve a diagnosis. On the other hand, we noticed in the medical maintenance category the emergence of a new set of problems for the doctor connected with the task of checking with wiser parents and the need for openness compared with the ambiguity which surrounds cases which are transitional between health and abnormal categories. These ambiguities are highlighted further in the receptive form of medicine practised with handicapped children described in the next chapter.

6

Serious Doubts

Previous chapters have described settings where the main concern of the medical work was to create and maintain a definition of normal childhood, though sometimes this normality was tempered by the recognition of clinical signs of abnormality. In the settings where initiative medicine was practised, parents' doubts and uncertainties were addressed by doctors in ways that attempted to convey a picture of childhood normality. In the settings where receptive medicine was practised, tight control was exercised over the admission of children to a patient or sick role. Where physical abnormality was identified, as positive a version of normal childhood as possible was evoked by the doctors. The setting that is described in this chapter differed in many significant respects from the other settings, mainly because it dealt with children whose normality was called into question, which had serious implications for their future identities as 'normal' people. Unlike the other settings, this particular clinic's work potentially involved the recruitment of some children to a handicapped identity and in managing the transition from the identity of 'normal' or 'ill' child to a stigmatic and socially spoiled 'handicapped' identity, a transition that was medically irreversible. This chapter then is concerned to show the ways in which the medical work performed and its setting together created a context in which this difficult transition was routinely effected. This is not to say that these were a particularly conscious or well thought out set of deliberate strategies by the doctors. Like much of the activity described in other chapters, it was more a matter of the ways in which a number of features together produced a *context* that created dilemmas for those working in them and that made some actions more likely to resolve them then others. The consequence was that medical and parental doubts about the child's normality were reinforced and maintained and a handicapped identity proffered. Such an identity implied repeated contact with medical services, and in some cases, the eventual surrender of the child to medical or social work control in the form of residential provision.

Referral

By the time children reached the clinic where developmental assessment was the main task, they were surrounded by considerable medical doubt, either coming directly from GP referrals or from re-referrals within the specialist clinic system. Like other diagnostic sessions, there was a presenting problem, either a medical suspicion that may not have been voiced, or a definite diagnosis of a physical impairment that might have wider implications for the child's normality. Either way, the parent arrived at the clinic aware that something was, or might be, seriously wrong with the child. Instead of the premise of 'normality' that underlies the other receptive or screening sessions, the issue of 'normality' remained open in this particular setting and yet to be medically validated or invalidated.

There has been a long history of constructions of 'normal' development and of attempts to construct age graded norms for the organization of various capacities (Parmalee 1962). Even those that have wide usage have not been without their critics (Frankenberg *et al.* 1971; Barnes and Stark 1975).

The seriousness of the issues at stake was further heightened by the special arrangements that were made for the clinic. The typical sessions was about thirty to forty minutes long, the clinic load was lighter than other clinics because more had to be done and done in a thorough manner. The notes had to be gone through thoroughly and in some cases special searches mounted to locate the relevant maternity hospital records. The medical information they contained might well be crucial in reconstructing a detailed medical biography for the child. The construction of such medical histories did not always offer a clear-cut route to an unequivocal diagnosis. For the precise connections between obstetric complications and subsequent neurological development were not always obvious or well established (Roberts 1970).

The clinic dealt in matters that the doctors viewed as so emotionally charged that the clinic's use for teaching was not encouraged. Indeed when students did turn up, they proved a liability. With obvious distaste, the doctors would teach, but tried to segregate the teaching from the consultation itself. They rarely tried to use the child to demonstrate features to students. On the few occasions when it was done, it was a source of embarrassment to the doctor and of alarm to the mother, as information came out that might (and did) upset the mother.

Thus, during one session when the doctor invited another doctor to examine the child, the student announced he had heard a heart murmur. At this the mother went white and tense while the doctor in charge, in irritated fashion, had to spend some time reassuring the mother that it was benign and unimportant and in no way indicated yet a further abnormality in an already physically handicapped child. It was for these kinds of reasons that teaching was explicitly eschewed and the researchers were the only audience present, not requiring teaching or any other attention. The doctors felt mothers had enough to cope with without the interference of students.

This clinic also had a higher number of fathers and other relatives attending along with the mother and child than any other setting. The doubt was great, the family had a shared fate should their child turn out to be abnormal in some respect. Typically, fathers deferred to mothers on issues of child development, but were more often involved in asking for diagnoses and prognoses.

The clinic agenda

The agenda for clinics typically consisted of an opening, vague statement, e.g. 'There seems to be some worry about his sitting', in order to get the parent to reveal their concerns, worries, or stories about sitting, standing, feeding, and so on, to check what they had *already* been told. From this point the doctor then went back over the child's medical history in detail with the mother, usually checking the notes against the mother's answers, enquiring into illnesses in the neonatal period and any subsequent symptoms of anything out of the ordinary.

This opening sequence for new cases was important, for it was an indirect way in which the doctor could find out what the mother knew already, who had told her, and what they thought was wrong. It also enabled the doctor to assess the degree to which the mother accepted or doubted the reasons for referral to the clinic. It also enabled the doctor to assess how much the mother could take in the way of bad news if it had to be broken.

From there, the doctor went on to elicit a developmental history, asking at what ages children acquired various normal competences, smiling, sitting, standing, vocabulary, etc. There then followed a standard assessment of current capacities with each item being checked on a master development chart. These included standard tests for gross motor, fine motor, verbal, and social functioning to be performed in the clinic (Barnes and Stark 1975). Then a thorough physical examination would be conducted ending with notes being written up and a statement of findings being given. The sequence of activities as immutable, and like other diagnostic sessions information had to be produced in a form required by the doctor. Thus, while the mother might have well-turned stories to tell, these were really rather irrelevant for medical purposes; even if, for example, the history had been done several times before (as it had in most cases) it was still done in detail again; if others had tested the child the doctor still did it in great detail. Such thoroughness had obvious benefits. At the same time it indicated that the issue was of some seriousness.

In cases of suspected delay or retardation, or where the relationship between a physical impairment, e.g. spina bifida and hydrocephalous and intellectual functioning was in doubt, they were typically recalled. The clinic thus comprised mainly 'old' cases in various stages of recall. Such cases could be held for a long time. A child referred at the age of ten months could still be being seen three or four years later. Delay often had a complex aetiology (if it was established at all) and uncertain prognosis. Consequently, such cases were 'held' on review for long periods of time with uncertain diagnosis or prognosis.

Such uncertainty can create of doubt. In fact, a consequence of the work performed was to prepare in advance a situation in which 'bad news' was broken long before any overt verbal acknowledgement of 'bad news' took place.

Creating co-operation and assessing the child

Unlike the other settings, testing was a serius business. Children's co-operation was required, if not at once then certainly in the future. Children *had* to do tests as the results were crucial for diagnosis and prognosis. No assumption of competence or unvalidated report of competence sufficed.

The doctors used a variety of standardized test to examine the child's behaviour and abilities. However, before the doctors could make any judgements about the child, based on his or her performance, they had to know if the child was performing to the best of his or her ability. There were several possible responses by the child to the doctor's examination. They sometimes refused to co-operate, went dumb and limp, or alternatively fought and screamed. If the child did co-operate, it was sometimes in different ways from those desired, e.g. some treated the occasion as one of 'play' rather than a serious occasion. Thus one child simply repeated the doctor's questions and requests rather than 'answering' them; one child built bricks in a line rather than piling up; and others repeated parts of what they had been asked to do earlier.

In order for the tests to proceed effectively, the child had to be willing and able to accept the role of 'examinee'. This was not a role that children automatically knew how to play; some were unable to appreciate the significance of what was going on, some were bored, tired, frightened, or interested in other things. In the most extreme case they themselves claimed the role of examiner and cast the doctor as the examinee — this was one of the tactics used by an eight-year-old girl who refused to accept the definition of childhood described in Chapter 2. Instead, she asked the doctor questions about his instruments and commented upon his behaviour with, it appeared, the mother's approval.

At one level it is perhaps important that the child should not understand what is going on. The manner in which testing was carried out was fundamentally deceptive since it was presented to the child as almost totally non-judgemental. The doctor's whole style told the child there was nothing to worry about, that it did not matter if the child could not or would not do it; and yet every aspect of the child's behaviour was open to scrutiny and the judgements based thereon heavily influenced his or her future life.

Two further features that may have aided the child in its definition of the situation were the presence of both a 'tester' and of an 'audience'. The extent to which the mother intervened and took over the doctor's role in aiding, coaxing, and instructing the child during the tests varied greatly. The more this occurred, the more normal the situation may have appeared to the child — assuming that the mother had instructed and played with the child in the same way at home. Conversely, the less the mother intervened, the more she came to constitute an 'audience'. This effect was amplified if she had other children present to take care of as well, and these too may have constituted yet more onlookers and 'audiences'. Added to this, there was a permanent audience in the clinic of the two researchers as well as the staff nurse, and very occasionally medical students were present. All of these took a keen interest in the child and its activities. Thus, the orientation of those present to the child in a *central* manner put the child on the centre of the stage and produced a performance. This still left open what content the performance might have, which script would be followed, and with what desired effect.

Most young children appeared to spend a good deal of time trying to work out what sort of situation it might be. They inspected various features of the setting, in particular the toys, the doctor's instruments, the doctor, and the audience. They looked at them, pointed to them, talked to and about them. Such behaviour was used by the adults present in a variety of ways. On the one hand it was often medically relevant in itself. It may further medical ends, in that in this exploration the child may get used to his environment and therefore be more willing to co-operate; it can be played upon to aid the examination — children may be distracted during physical examination by the toys or by the audience smiling and playing with them. On the other hand this was not allowed to go too far, otherwise the testing would break down, e.g. some children became so involved in play as to make examination impossible.

Many parents were thus unwilling to let their children's engagement in the setting become too active. Some, however, encouraged this just so that the child could demonstrate how 'wonderful', etc. they were to the doctor, an act that children were, not unnaturally, quite keen to perform. Some parents and children reacted to the situation by going through the tricks that the parents adored. Such attempts were, of course, severely limited by the child's subordinate place within the clinic, but given doting parents it could succeed for considerable periods of time.

The doctor's attempts to structure the situation for the child involved a number of different strategies, such as locating the activity among a range of possible activities by comparing then contrasting it with other activities that he assumed were known by the child. Sometimes he formulated his own activity for the child, e.g. 'I'm just going to see what you can do with your hands', though for younger children this was normally said to the parents. Formulating the child's activity, and thus the expected identity, was done in a variety of ways, e.g. by comparing it to other activities — 'It's just like school, a game, isn't it?' — or by recognizing that it might seem odd — 'I'll ask you some funny things . . . What do you do when you feel cold?', or even positively wrong — 'You stare at him [one of the researchers during an eye-test], *it's not rude* — you stare at him'. All of these remarks were made to a shy, frightened eight-year-old.

The doctors used various tactics to define the test as a test and to tell children how to behave as a proper examinee. They asked questions, issued sets of rules and instructions which were continually repeated, and illustrated them themselves. They praised good test performances as performance — 'You're good at this bit, aren't you?' They informed them that the testing consisted of a variety of different activities, one after the other — 'Let's see, what can we get you to do next?' They also made notes in between and during the activities, and also watched the child's performance intently and closely.

To induce the children to perform, doctors offered them a very distinctive and intensive style of interaction. They went to considerable lengths to smooth the interaction to make it as interesting and cheerful as possible, giving a running commentary on every aspect. They checked that the child was sitting comfortably, that they were not wearing anything too tight or too hot, that they were not distracted by other things. They demonstrated close interest in the child's activities, getting very close to them, looking into their eyes, speaking in a soft, gentle tone, making conversation about what they took to be the child's *participation* in the actual tests with constant praise, while never or very rarely implying any criticisms. Unlike the other clinics though, this praise was limited to *specific* competences, it was not directed at the whole child. Indeed there was a marked refusal to wonder at the children in the clinic. Praise, wonder, and joy in this clinic were restricted in their use to occasions when it was quite clear that parents shared the doctor's view of the childs problems, so that it became praise and wonder within a very different version of childhood (Davis and Strong 1976). They made slow, deliberate movements and similarly always spoke very slowly and carefully. They did not get cross with a failure to respond, instead they merely repeated the test instructions or varied slightly their instructions using exactly the same gentle quiet tones. If there was still no response, they moved, without expressing regret, onto another task. At the same time they might put on a performance themselves to amuse the child; they joked, made fools of themselves, and minimized their own ability at the task in, for example hopping across the clinic on one foot or kicking a ball, all to encourage the child to compete and excel.

In ensuring the child's co-operation, the doctor was centrally faced not just with manipulating the child, but also the parents (this, of course, usually meant the mother). Given the importance of the parents as the child's major reality-definers, the doctor also enlisted their help in defining for the child the activities in which they were to engage.

Parents initially differed greatly in their conceptions of appropriate parental identities. Some intervened in the testing too much, usurping both the doctor's and the child's role, asking the child too many questions, prompting his answers or indeed answering the questions that the doctor had put to the child. Some defined the clinic as purely the doctor's affair and sat upright and apart, never coming to the doctor's or child's assistance unless

asked to do so. Some, mainly middle-class, allowed their children to
rampage through the clinic, disturbing files, rolling on the floor,
climbing on trolleys, etc. Some tried to redefine the whole occasion
as one where the parents and child demonstrate to the doctor how
wonderful, adoring, cute, etc. they are. Others went to the opposite
extreme and totally browbeat their children during the clinic,
monitoring all their behaviour, threatening them, adjusting their
clothing and appearance and, on occasion, attempting to enlist the
doctor's aid in the control of the child at home as well as in the
clinic, e.g. over 'smoking' or 'too much television'.

Such variation in behaviour was perhaps more characteristic of
parents and children in their first few contacts with the doctor.
Parents who had been in repeated contact for some time were more
likely to know what to expect, the identities that best fitted the
clinic agenda and doctor's task (those of 'aides' and 'detached
observers') and when the child would be required to perform and at
what. Repeated contact shaped and firmed up the divergent initial
definitions of appropriate parental behaviours into one predom-
inant form that meshed with the doctor's expectations. In short,
they assumed their role.

The main point in going into co-operation at length has been to
show it to be a central and continual concern of the doctor. Given
that the adjudication of the doctor on the child's identity was partly
based on test performance, it was obviously of considerable
concern that the doctor should actually elicit a performance. While
in other settings refusal might be accepted or glossed over as
unimportant, that the doctors spent so much time enlisting parents
and the child's co-operation marked the setting off as special and
unique. Such protracted warming-in was not a particularly
noticeable feature of the other settings.

A further point to note is the *extent* to which the child was tested.
In this setting, unlike others, the child's competences were
systematically tested, then broken down into a set of component
parts to produce a new assembly, a medical version of the child's
identity. Such dismantling of the child on medical criteria, not
common-sense or lay criteria, reinforced both the mysteriousness
of medicine and the potential strangeness of the child along a set
of dimensions hitherto unknown to the parents.

While in other settings such testing was also done, it was not so
thorough or deemed so essential that it was worth persisting with if
the child did not perform or resisted. The breaking down of the
child into component parts, each one to be demonstrated, did not
occur to the same extent.

It has been noted that the child's behaviour in the clinic may be partly a product of the novelty of the situation, of how the child and parents define the setting. Doctors routinely made allowances for the possible effects of context on performance during testing. However, for the parents it was often an issue of some importance. For it provided an account for the child's failure to perform the tests, and also to discredit the doctor's typification of the child based on those tests. The clinic's effect on children's behaviour (and also parents, adults, doctors, strangers, etc.) could constitute a resource for them as well as the doctor. Sometimes they attempted to reinforce or discredit the evidence of the child's clinic behaviour by, for example, pointing out the typicality of some features, downplaying others, coaxing, praising, and encouraging some actions while ignoring others; and on one occasion telling the doctor not to believe a word the child said. In this particular case the mother started off by telling the doctor not to believe what her son said since he always said 'yes' to doctors. A few minutes later she called him an 'actor' and a 'joker' and said sharply to the child upon the doctor's final question to the child, 'Don't lie'!

Testing the parents

Unlike the other settings, the parents' answers to questions were not assumed to be accurate, truthful, or disinterested. Parents were on trial too.

Parents may not, in fact, have been particularly attentive observers of their children's behaviour — especially if they themselves had had no worries about the child. Those who had studied their children closely may have had great difficulty in describing or remembering medically crucial incidents or behaviour. Parents usually had commonsense and not medical criteria for what was 'memorable' and thus 'to be remembered'. Where two parents turned up it would often require mother and father to negotiate the place of events in the child's biography.

Even where parents could describe in detail, they were uncertain as to what was wanted. The doctor's questions may not have made sense, or may have been too vague. Added to this, of course, were the typical communication problems caused by differences in class, sub-culture, education, and so on. Parents differed greatly in their ability to give detailed descriptions in a concise and coherent manner — partly through variation in skill and partly in confidence. These problems were, for medical purposes, all of a kind. The doctor still faced the problem of turning all lay stories into relevant medical data. The elaborate detail from a middle-class mother had to be condensed, while the uncommunicative working-class mother's stories required amplification. Both demanded translation to medical relevancies.

Further, parents as well as doctors were diagnosticians; if they thought there was a 'problem' then they too would elaborate a commonsense etiology, symptomatology, diagnosis, prognosis, and possible course of treatment, if any. Such elaboration would continue after attendance at numerous clinics, particularly since the doctor rarely would or could provide a final and elaborate etiology, diagnosis, or prognosis. Thus, the parents' observation of the child and their recollection of his past were guided by their current analysis. A considerable distortion could result. For example, two mothers of suspected epileptic children both initially placed the onset of the attacks prior to the date the doctor eventually decided upon. Both had been worried for a long time whether they should see their doctor about the child. When they did go, and epilepsy was suspected, they both evidenced considerable guilt at having 'delayed'. Delay took its meaning from the time of diagnosis, which exists in 'medical' time but not necessarily in 'lay' time.

Objective testing and examination gives the doctor data on the child that has not passed through a filter of parental interpretation. However, this was still often influenced by the parents and the context. With young children there were all sorts of problems in interpreting the results of such tests, the same problems that the doctor encountered in observing the child's behaviour in the clinic. It left unanswered the question of the typicality of the behaviour and left problematic the effect of the context of the testing and observation on the child's performance on any one test. Consequently, the doctor was forced initially to rely largely on the information that the parents produced in assessing the child's status and conferring on them an expertise about the child that enabled them to challenge him in many ways. The doctor was put in a position of continually asking for information and for interpretations of the child's behaviour e.g. 'How many words can he speak?'; 'Is he putting words together yet?'; 'What did that [child's noise] mean?'; 'Can he do this at home?'. Reliance on parents' stories diminished the more contact the doctor had with the child. For the first couple of sessions parental observation was often at a premium in cases of suspected delay.

As often happened, the child either performed the tests in a desultory fashion, did not perform at all, or was so disruptive that the physical examination was curtailed, the doctor became completely dependent on the parents' replies. As well as assessing the child he had to assess the credibility of the parents.

In the formulation of questions, the doctor was at a disadvantage in that the detailed daily activities of the child were unavailable to him and he therefore had to question the parents in the most general and decontextualised terms. The parents in turn were able to supply the context in replying to questions, and sometimes did so in great detail, giving out a welter of stories, examples, and explanations in response to questions like 'How has he been doing since I last saw you?', and 'How have things been going on?'. This gave the parents a stock of information that could be, and was, used to discredit the doctor's typification of the child, e.g.:

(D) 'His hands are very trembly.' (Observing child stacking building bricks)
(M) 'It's only when he's involved in something or when he's excited about something — he's not trembly *all* the time.'

    or

(D) 'Can he walk upstairs on his own?'
(M) 'No, I've never seen him.'
(D) 'He can't?'
(M) 'We haven't got any stairs in our house, it's a flat, all on one floor.'

    or (the doctor observing child's 'difficulty' in throwing a ball)

(D) 'He's not very good at that, is he?'
(M) 'He doesn't play with a *small* ball, he has a *big* beach ball he plays with all the time at home.'

The doctor was thus confronted with persons who claimed an expert knowledge of the child. He had to consult them in order to become an expert on the child himself. The expertise of the parents was not disinterested in the ways in which the doctor's was, so he was continually on his guard as to whether they were painting 'too rosy a picture' of the child's abilities. A key aspect of this was the extent to which the parents talked about their child as data, as detached observers who reported reliably on the child's *failures* as well as successes. An anxious over-involvement with the child was taken as a sign that the mother's account was biased in the child's favour.

A further difficulty for the doctor was that the mother was often in contact with a number of professionals, e.g. social workers, physiotherapists, opthalmologists, etc., who all supplied the mother with information that could be fed back into the clinic at later visits, e.g.:

(D) 'There was some trouble with his hearing last time.'
(M) 'The ear doctor tested him and said he was all right.'
(D) (Looks in notes to see if there is a report)

Where the mothers had some professional expertise (e.g. teachers, nurses) the doctor was more likely to accept their accounts of the child as having some basis in a body of knowledge or experience, and they in turn were more likely to give highly qualified and detailed answers to his questions and invoke other authorities. The most 'difficult' cases were ones where the mother was unforthcoming or monosyllabic in her replies, as this led to difficulty in assigning any significance to the mother's replies to decontextualised questions.

The most difficult of all were the ones who claimed the *same* medical expertise as he did. In one extreme case, the mother was a nurse who systematically devastated the ways in which the doctor normally controlled the clinic. She indicated that she had once been a nurse and proceeded to pull out of her bag a sheet of paper that contained the complete medical history of her large family. She proceeded to read it out very quickly. She used a battery of medical terms, and refused to describe possible and epileptic attacks so that the doctor could interpret them. He attempted to discredit her use of the terms by asking her to describe 'What *you* call "*petit mal*" attacks'. She used medical terminology through the session and referred to her paediatric nursing as giving her an authoritative body of knowledge on which to base her remarks. She refused to subscribe to the doctor's format, causing him continually to try to slow her down, saying 'Wait a minute', 'Hold on', 'Can you go back a bit?' 'No, don't tell me about the second one — I want to hear about the first one', etc. She commented to the child and the doctor on the tests as he performed them, indicating her knowledge, and was able to tell the child what would happen next. She asked the doctor questions that implied shared medical knowledge. At one point she dropped her sheet of paper. The exasperated doctor commented, 'You've dropped your script!', which led her into a forceful statement about the need for good records, in which the doctor shamefacedly acquiesced.

In this case, the mother's claim disconcerted the doctor and left him embarrassed and annoyed at her self-confident claims. While this type of thing was unusual in such an extreme form, it does indicate that the doctor's expertise was sometimes fragile and subject to assault in the clinic.

As a consequence of such problems the doctors seemed not to trust the parents' story, at least initially. Rather, as we noted earlier, expertise on the parents' part has to be earned and doctors used a variety of tactics to determine their credibility and accuracy as observers, and to improve their observation. Suspicions about the former were, of course, rarely manifested, rather a friendly but formal air was maintained throughout (Strong and Davis 1978).

One of the main disadvantages that the doctor faced, the fact that parents did not normally know what was medically relevant, was also an advantage as far as testing their credibility went. The doctor's 'hidden agenda', the fact that he knew what was and was not medically likely, allowed him to check their story in ways that were not available to them and therefore could not be incorporated by them (Scheff 1968).

The doctor was never, however, completely reliant upon a single story from the mother. A medically relevant story was elicited in a number of ways. First, the doctor used his authority to structure the content and course of conversation. He defined himself as the questioner and selected what was 'important' in the parents' reply. Parents were rarely left to tell their story at their own pace and in their own way. The exceptions were revealing. The doctor often issued a vague invitation to tell a story at the beginning of the clinic — 'How's X been doing?', 'What seems to have been the trouble?'. However, since it was not specified what would count as an appropriate answer to this, many parents let this go, leaving the doctor free to move in and ask more precise questions. Lengthy stories only got told (a) where the doctor was completely dependent on information from parents which could not be cross-checked, e.g. description of epileptic attacks; (b) where the parents were very worried; (c) where the doctor defined the parent as an expert; (d) where the doctor was out-numbered — if both parents appeared and both were determined to tell a story then he was usually constrained to listen to it. Apart from these exceptions, parents did not have the chance to present a coherent story, and even when they did so the doctor, as we shall see, proceeded to take it apart. Any story enabled the doctor to do a great deal of internal cross-checking, by repeatedly going over the same ground but from slightly different angles.

A second way in which the doctor escaped reliance upon the parents' story was by drawing upon data from other sources. As well as his own observations in the clinic he had the medical record of the child, and the observations of other doctors, social workers, physiotherapists, GPs, etc. They were in some cases supplemented by case conferences (from which parents were excluded) on particularly problematic children. Though using these sources has its own drawbacks, their very multiplicity enabled cross-checking.

Thus, the doctor often asked parents for information which he already had from other sources. Questions to the mother about the child's vocabulary were checked against what the child said in the clinic. The results of testing particular skills in the clinic could be extrapolated to check on similar skills mentioned by the parents.

That such cross-checking was possible obviously acted as a constraint upon the parents, and was visibly signified to the parents by the open file for the child, which the doctor consulted frequently. On occasion he spelled this out to the parents, e.g. in one case the mother had been causing the GP 'trouble', the GP had written to the doctor to this effect, and the doctor initiated the interaction by saying, 'I've got a letter from your doctor and I gather there's been some trouble over [the nature of the disagreement]'.

Such letters were private communications between doctors; parents were never told the content of the letters except in extreme cases, for example, to convince anxious parents that nothing was being hidden from them and that everyone was doing their best to achieve a diagnosis, or where some course of action was overtly contingent upon a third party's advice or decision. Normally though, the medical record, referral notes, documents, and reports were seen only by doctors. This constituted a formidable hidden resource.

Further, given the doctor's licence as an expert to test the child then he could choose to exercise this to check the mother's story, e.g. questions about whether the child could jump or stand on one leg were often followed by attempts to test just this. Finally, given that the bulk of the cases dealt with in the clinic were developmental ones, almost any aspect of child's behaviour could be deemed relevant. Thus, all interaction involving the child in the clinic was in some sense a 'test'. The doctor tested the child while apparently merely being friendly and saying, 'Hello', or 'Goodbye'; nor was the mother's interaction with the child immune from inspection. Even the apparently non-medical parts of the encounter could be inspected on medical grounds.

So far the discussion has presupposed that the parents had a story to tell. Of course, one of the major problems was that very often they had not, or even if they had, it was not the one the doctor wanted to hear. Doctors, therefore, had a variety of techniques for eliciting information. As regards the format of the questions these were often fairly vague initialy, merely naming some activity and asking the parents, 'Can he do X?'. Further questions would be elaborated if the parent merely answered 'Yes' or 'No' and failed to specify 'how' and 'in what circumstances'; for fairly precise information was wanted even if this was not indicated in the initial question; the instructions to parents about what counted as an adequate answer were only implicit; parents had to pick them up as they went along.

Even when the parents did talk, their meaning was not always clear, but persistent asking for elaboration was one way of getting at meanings. For example, in the following extract from a case of a retarded four-year-old boy the doctor is trying to establish the extent of the child's soiling:

(D) 'And has he *ever* been reliably dry night and day?'
(M) 'Well he *never* wets himself.'
(D) 'And when's that been since ... since *when*?'
(M) 'I think it was two and a half.'
(D) 'Uh-huh — and this soiling problem — has it *always* been there?'
(M) 'Well this is it, he doesn't *always* empty his bowel all at one.'
(D) 'U-huh — so how *often* is he messing his pants?'
(M) 'Well — not for the last four days.'
(D) 'But how *often*?'
(M) 'Well ... up to three times a day, when he is with his dad he goes well his dad's a long distance lorry driver, but he won't for me. He was all right when he was with his dad on holiday, but he's not now ...' (doctor switches topic)

In just the same way as the doctor has technical terms not available to the parents which he must explain to them, so may the parents have their own vocabulary for describing illness and behaviour.

When the parents had a well-turned story to tell and the doctor was willing or forced to let them tell it, then he faced the task of transforming it into medically relevant data. A variety of techniques were used here. Firstly, the doctor structured the story by reinforcing the parts he thought were crucial, only certain parts were written up or commented upon. In line with this the doctor asked the parents to go over *selected* points in much greater detail, which broke the story up into sections. Finally, the doctor attempted to rework the story once it has been completed and to produce his own medically relevant version, selected and ordered by the principles of his medical agenda. Although the story was re-cast in terms of his medical purposes, it was still told in the parents' terminology so that they can check upon its accuracy. The story was retold in stages and after each stage the doctor sought the parents' assent. This repetition occurred on a much smaller scale during routine questioning of the parents. Sometimes the doctor attempted to sum up the results of a whole section of questions, and he typically repeated a parent's answers to each question to make sure *he* had got it right, that the *parent* has got it right, and that 'it' now has the status of a shared, established fact, e.g.

(D) 'What happens then?'
(M) 'She goes stiff.'
(D) 'She goes stiff?'
(M) 'Yes.'
(D) 'Uh-huh.' (writes in records and switches topic)

Despite this variety of resources and techniques, the doctor's scope for checking was fairly limited. Communication with colleagues by letter suffered the same sorts of communication problems as the doctor/parent interaction while it was of necessity much briefer. Although the case notes on a child might be highly detailed, much of this was irrelevant for present purposes while they grew to such mountainous proportions (as the most aware parents pointed out) that they forced the doctor to rely on summaries and these had their own inaccuracies. The background data that the doctor had on parents was severely limited, though social workers might be used particularly in problematic cases to fill this out, and the doctor had little time to get know the parents himself. This time-limit also prevented systematic cross-checking. Many more of the parents' statements could have been checked out in the clinic than in fact were. There was also the central constraint that the doctor's suspicions about the parents' accuracy must not become too obvious. Since the doctor often had very little to offer the parents, to make his interrogative tactics too overt would be to threaten the parents' co-operation and even attendance at the clinic.

Despite this there were various features with which the doctors could console themselves. Most of the cases in the clinic were defined as long-term ones for whom no immediate decision was medically vital. The major decision-point was often not until the start of schooling at five years of age, and the doctor would see a child on many occasions before that. Present omissions and mistakes could therefore be corrected in the future without too much harm being done. Since this was so, and since the doctor used standard sets of questions, he had the opportunity to train the parents up into the kinds of ideal observer he would like them to be. Such training was rarely explicit; rather, parents were given the repeated opportunity to observe which features the doctors typically asked questions about, express surprise at, take notes upon, summarize, etc. Once the parent had learned these, then the question and answer routines became far more fluent — in some cases the doctor needed only to ask one question of the parent to provide detailed answers to both this and the questions that normally followed it. Further, the more the parent accepted the medical definition of the child, then the more able they were to move away from the 'proud parent' role to that of 'detached observer'. Thus, persuading parents to accept his diagnosis and prognosis was also central to his transforming them into his 'medical aides' (Strong and Davis 1978).

The most noteworthy feature of this degree of thoroughness was that is served to call into doubt that parents' claims for their children could be taken at their face value and left at that. In the other settings we noted that the parents' answers to doctors' questions were typically taken as non-problematic, that they were adequate, true, and indicative of a correct concern to praise the child. Here, instead, stories were subject to vigorous testing, multiple sources of evidence were used, and seemingly adequate answers subject to demand for further specification, contextual elaboration to get beneath the normal everyday terms in which parents described their children to a more important and hidden medically relevant set of 'facts'. Again this served to call into permanent doubt whether the parents had really appreciated the fact that something might be seriously wrong with their child and to signal that they themselves were indirectly under inspection. While this never led to any great display of hostility on the parents' part, many responded in an uneasy fashion, their competence as parents called into sudden doubt.

Telling

Telling 'bad news' was seen as a problem in this setting, whereas in the others, medical news usually did not have very damaging implications for the child's future. There are a number of reasons why 'telling' bad news appeared to be so difficult for the doctors and why they were so reluctant to do it. Telling 'good news' on the other hand was made much easier. The very thoroughness of the testing, checking, and recalls, as well as the authority of the specialist worked together to give considerable credibility to such 'good news'. For example in one case after three forty-minute sessions the doctor pronounced finally:

(D) 'Well, she's come on very well. I don't think we need to see her again ... she *has* come on ... she *has* improved.'
(M) 'Oh, that's such a relief!'

(D) 'Yes, well that's fine then' etc.
No questioning of the doctor ensued.

Thus, some children were discharged, authoritatively pro-nounced 'normal', to the evident relief of parents. Some, however, were discharged with their future left somewhat open. 'Good news' was heavily qualified. For example, some children were discharged, but with the proviso that they would never be 'likely to set the Thames on fire', would be at 'the bottom of the range', and 'not going to do as well at school as the other children'. In such cases the child was discharged with a provisional identity of 'normal' but that normality was to be further tested by the other institutions in our society, particularly the education system. Parents were exhorted 'not to push' such children, but to 'try and bring him on a bit' by enrolling children at nursery schools. In short, a degree of doubt was maintained though it was not deemed of sufficient magnitude to warrant further follow-up.

The discharges of old severely handicapped children were made to other caring institutions or professions that took over the medical management of the handicapped child on a residential or permanent basis. The rest were recalled over a long period of time to undergo the transitiòn from 'normal' to 'handicapped' identity.

Bad news was difficult to break because there was no specific medical remedy to follow on from the disclosure of bad news. The breaking of such news indicated medicine's impotence and also removed the case from traditional medical legitimation. For if there were no remedies, then what more could medicine do? To disclose such news moved the case into the permanently mentally or physically handicapped category where medical involvement was of a weak form — care rather than cure. The medical emphasis would, in these cases,be placed on 'management' and 'containment' of the effects of handicap, not just on the child but on the family as well, an area of involvement for which doctors are neither well trained nor ideally located.

Second, such bad news fundamentally assaults the normality of the child. It potentially obliterates other identities and com-monsense dictates it will be destructive for the family (Voysey 1975). The doctor, then, was an unwilling and reluctant change agent.

Third, the outcome of such bad news was unpredictable — some parents might at last be relieved to be released from a definitional limbo, but others might resist or reject the news. The doctor was in no position to enforce his own preferred outcome on the family as his particular authority stopped at the clinic door.

Fourth, doctors are ill-trained in making such revelations or coping with their consequences. While it can be done perhaps more easily if there is no continuing responsibility for the outcome of 'bad news', where the doctor has to break bad news in the context of an obligation to continue in contact, then such news can threaten the viability of the relationship for such management and counselling purposes as are possible. Typically, though, in the UK there was restricted opportunity for parents to shop around for another opinion (unlike the USA) so that the parties were bound together for some period of time.

Not surprisingly, the marked interest of doctors in communication could be reinterpreted as reflecting doctors' inability to control many other more important things for patients. If you cannot control or cure, e.g. the family environment or the child, then all you can deal with is what is under your control, namely your own words. Perhaps the communication literature's focus on why patients do not hear things or do not do as they are told owes more to the limitations of medicine than the limitations of patients.

There were however a number of ways in which the potential shock of the revelation of serious retardation or handicap was lessened. To begin with, the context for breaking bad news had often already been constructed. This was done in a number of ways. The long-term medical relationship that was developed over repeated recalls itself moved the child into a medically ambiguous category, particularly when it was *not* accompanied by the normalization typical in the other form of medical maintenance described in earlier chapters. All was not well, and what is more, what was wrong was not handled in a manner to separate it from the child's essential nature. Similarly, the tone of the clinic — thoroughly neutral, demanding accuracy of answers, the doctor's refusal to marvel at the child — worked to create medical ambiguity. The repetition of tests over and over again served to demonstrate in a visible manner that the child was not progressing. If there were other children in the family, the elongation of medical time also served to give the family time to compare their child with others.

The doctors also routinely refused, or were not able, to give clear diagnoses or prognoses, preferring to 'wait and see', for 'only time will tell'. Thus, these features taken together created a context in which the actual telling lost a lot of its significance, for the ground had already been well prepared. Nevertheless, many parents put up a rearguard action once the diagnosis was out in the open. For as we noted before, there was usually sufficient ambiguity for the parents to claim that their version of the child as normal was correct. Thus, parents would typically 'claim' their children were progressing, that they *could* do things at home that they 'wouldn't' do in the clinic. Such resistance, however, was gradually undermined by the continued overt demonstration of children's incompetence in clinic and forcing parents to agree that they could see it too. Thus, children's limitations, often *demonstrated* by the doctor, served to show the parents that his typification of the child was correct.

At this point it was perfectly possible for parents to 'appear' to 'accept' the doctor's news for their clinic attendance, but to hang on to hope privately, by engaging in attempts to coach the child, seek nursery care 'to bring him on', and speech therapy 'to help him with his talking'. Hope was transferred to other specialists, to physiotherapists to make the child walk, to speech therapists to make them talk, to teachers 'to help them learn'. As these were tried, in turn the doctor again had to try to reduce the parents' expectations, pointing out that either referral was a waste of time, which meant going over the ground again, or that while such referrals would be made, only marginal alleviation should be expected. Periodically the temporary definitional truce, the apparent working consensus, would be shattered by a question about normal schooling or a statement that a 'new' treatment was going to be tried (e.g. Philadelphia method). Such breaches were dealt with tactfully, for it was held to be reasonable that desperate parents would try anything to make their child 'normal', while statements about schooling would be received with concern, but with no encouragement. That parents 'hoped' that when the child was assessed for schooling at the age of five, a miracle would by then have occurred was accepted by the doctor who usually sympathetically said it was unlikely, as 'there are no miracles here', but anyway the decision was not theirs to make.

Perhaps the most crucial point at which serious conflict could have broken out between parent and doctor was over educational placement at the age of five. Here, though, the hospital doctors were able to disengage themselves from the decision made by another branch of the service, a Local Authority Medical Officer and Psychologist. Such a decision was presented as theirs to make by right and all the doctor could do was 'guess' what they 'might' say. Should the decision be one the parents disliked, the doctor could retain his relationship with them, commiserating and listening to their criticism of other branches of the service. He was not involved. In this case, the option was always left open that the doctor *might* be wrong, but that the likelihood was that the local authority doctor and psychologists would recommend special schooling. This outcome was also presented as 'in the child's best interests', for special schooling meant expert teachers and treatment facilities. The stigma of 'the feel school' (special school for the mentally and physically handicapped), was directly attacked and such establishments were praised for the care they took of difficult and troublesome children who 'wouldn't fit easily' in the normal classroom.

As we have noted elsewhere, the doctors' failure to marvel constituted a powerful indicator that all was not well (Davis and Strong 1976). Unlike the normal consultation, where there was no reason to marvel because the context was one of limited doubt, or the 'initiative' mode where there was every reason to recreate normality, in the special clinic it was *parents* who sought normality by trying to display their children to the doctors. While the doctors were not hostile to such attempts, they did not often honour them by joining in. Thus parents' attempts to praise the child, to get the child to do 'tricks', and to comment on moods, fads, and motives were politely noted but not agreed with. They were merely noted or the parents cautioned not to expect too much too soon. Some features were safe to comment on though, 'nice dresses', changes in 'hairstyles', comments on birthdays and age and holidays were safe topics of conversation. But these were things provided *for* the child which stemmed more from the mother's heroic activities and her concern for the child than from the child itself. They could be commented on because they were not topics indicating an essential normality which inhered within the child. They were epipheno-menal and not essential; appearances, not reality. Similarly the achievement of some basic competencies, even if they were still age inappropriate, could occasion joy and pleasure for both doctor and parent, but they could only be appreciated if both already agreed on the doctor's version of the child.

Once an apparent consensus had been reached where both doctor and parents agreed that the child was 'abnormal' then comments could be made, but they took their meaning from the centrality of the handicap identity. Such children could even be seen to be doing quite well, but in doing quite well they started from a very different set of standards which informed such a judgement. Praise of a child achieving continence meant something very different if the child in question was a four-year-old with severe spina bifida.

Within such a consensus parents were praised for their efforts on the child's behalf, for the burdens they were shouldering, and for the way in which they were co-operating with different services that were involved with parent and child. Indeed, such parents were welcomed to the clinic, for attending it sometimes appeared an irrelevant and onerous duty, particularly when little was achieved except a further check on no progress. Doctors often apologized for the imposition of such recalls, for the time the parents spent waiting outside the clinic, for bureaucratic muddles over referrals to other specialists.

The rare displays of emotion occurred amongst such 'heroes' whose coping was stretched to its limits. The doctor was sympathetic, but indicated there was not much that he could do. The *lack* of open emotion was interesting. The literature abounds in 'horror stories' yet we noticed little overt display of extreme emotion in the setting. The explanation for this lies perhaps in Voysey's argument that such parents are 'forced' to display their competence in extreme circumstances (Voysey 1975). Couple this with the sympathetic neutrality of the doctors and the neutral frame they sought to establish, and the lack of display of emotion was explicable, particularly given the clinic's concentration on the management of mundane affairs like schooling, day care, eating, and other daily activities. The full story of the parents' feelings was never required at any one time — rather it was everyday coping that was at issue. As one mother remarked when asked how she was coping, 'Well — you just take it day by day, don't you'. The doctor's refusal to treat handicapped children as 'altars' on which parents 'sacrificed' themselves also indicated a moral imperative. Such children were people to be 'managed' and not to be objects of distaste or horror as common sense dictates. This too neutralized the expression of extreme emotions. The children became strategic problems in which the parents and the doctor could collaborate.

Assessing responsibility

As I have argued in Chapter 2, the child is not usually viewed as a competent member. This means that others, particularly parents, assume responsibilities in relation to the child. In some situations this allocation of responsibilities is called into question. One such situation is when the child is labelled as 'disabled', 'retarded', or 'mentally defective' in the course of medical treatment. Other situations leading to a redistribution of responsibility exist apart from the medical situation, for example, when a child is taken into care by the social work authority or when guardians are legally appointed in the event of the death of the parents.

In the clinics attended, the participants often made reference to the question of responsibility, in particular to the extent to which parents were prepared or expected by doctors to be responsible for the child, the extent to which the doctors were willing to assume responsibility for the child, and how far the child was responsible for its own actions.

These questions as they emerged were settled in different ways depending on the type of ailment that was diagnosed. Thus, for the short illness episode the question of responsibilities seemed most clear-cut. The parents assumed that they would continue to act as parents for the foreseeable future, the doctor accepted responsibility for medical treatment for the child, but limited this to specific and narrow intervention. Most were referred back to their GP for treatment on the understanding that they would only be referred again if the condition failed to respond to treatment. The extent of the child's responsibility for his actions was rarely raised as a problem.

In the case of children who were diagnosed as 'retarded', 'backward', or 'disabled', the issues were much less clear-cut. In such cases the doctor usually deferred a prediction of the child's future condition, in some cases telling the parents he was not yet prepared to answer their questions on this subject. Also, the parents were unsure about the likely outcome, and so what usually occurred was that over a period of visits to the clinic the parents and doctor engaged in a process of testing each other out to see how the other party viewed the future of the child. There were no cures for most of these conditions, indeed there was often no clear aetiology either. The key decision which faced both doctor and parent was what would happen when the child was of school age; and the pressure was on both doctor and parent to have made a decision about the child before the issue of schooling becomes a reality.

The clinic agenda was consequently much wider than in the other settings, potentially encompassing all the aspects of family life that had a bearing on the treatment of the handicapped child. Rather than doctors stating that these *were* their concerns, they indicated by general questions, e.g. 'And how are things at home?', or 'How are you coping?', that if the parents wished they could put them on the agenda.

In the following example the doctor comments on a three-year-old girl with severe metabolic disorder who has, in the clinic, gone wild, screamed and fought and (unusually) has been slapped by her father.

> (D) 'She's always on the go isn't she? Is she always like
>   this? I mean, is this typical — it's not just this
>   afternoon?'
> (M and F) 'It's typical.'

(D) 'And you can cope?'
(F) 'Yes.'
(M) 'You get used to it.'

Moralizing was eschewed, as was any attempt at moral inspection, even where home circumstances were known to be less than ideal. Such problems were the province of the hospital social workers rather than the doctor. Thus, reported difficulties in coping were sympathetically received, but with no hint of any judgement of dereliction of parental duty, or fecklessness.

Similarly, the doctors who worked in this clinic more than any other also had to contend with continual sniping, anger, and indication of dissatisfaction with what was being done (or was not being done) for their child. This put the doctor in the invidious position where any of his statements could be taken as validation of such criticism. Interestingly, the doctors allowed the expression of the criticism, but did not validate it by agreeing that such criticism was correct. Instead, the doctors indicated that they could *understand* why such criticism was being made. After all, it provided evidence that the parents were correctly concerned with getting the maximum benefit they could for their child. Such criticism was further legitimated by the doctors themselves who cast themselves in the role of concerned but relatively helpless allies of the parents. Thus doctors would confess to ignorance of aetiology, prognosis, an ignorance that was not personal but shared by the profession as a whole in face of chronic, incapacitating conditions.

Such ignorance was tempered by moral concern and a recognition that other specialities could effect some improvement. Other services were praised by the doctor even when they too had failed to produce a miracle. Criticism might be onerous, but it was reasonable from parents with handicapped children. In any case, the doctors were rarely in a position to intervene as advocates for the parents. Their authority was limited to the clinic and the hospital. Also, the doctors were invariably one amongst many involved in the case, but not in charge of the team. They too had to respect the given hospital division of labour and prestige in such cases.

For example, in the long-term cases, the GPs rights in the case were always respected. After each consultation, a letter would be sent to the GP telling him what had occurred, what had been found or recommended, and informing him that the child would be seen again in three month's time. Yet it was quite striking how few parents mentioned the GP at hospital consultations. A wide range of others, speech therapists, psychologist, surgeons, (orthopaedic, opthalmic, and ENT), social workers, and therapists were mentioned, but rarely the GP. The GP also rarely turned up at hospital case conferences on such children, indicating that such cases were firmly the province of specialist services. Scheduling contact with this multiplicity of persons and organizations often defeated the doctor, as he openly admitted.

Not surprisingly, the work-up done on 'new' and 'old' patients' notes was usually done to establish the current state of the field of other workers currently involved in the case. The 'work-up' of the notes was devoted largely to establishing sequences of events for long-term and complicated cases. These were often difficult to check; records were incomplete, referrals initiated but no report of any contact from the specialist involved, and sometimes no indication of the outcome of such meetings.

For example, the doctor's opening remarks during the work-up of one set of notes went like this:

(D) 'The next one is X. I've not seen him before — has been referred by Specialist Y, he's three-and-a-quarter now — em — em — he was said, six months ago, to be slow and clumsy — oh — it's *just* like Specialist Y — no diagnosis and no help — who *else* is involved — occupational therapy — "query retarded" — oh — em — his *hearing* has been checked, that's all right, though there was a lot of doubt about deafness — Specialist 2 said he was deaf but on follow-up he was all right. Ah! *two* reports from occupational therapy, but I don't think anyone's done a birth and development history — um — Specialist Y never wrote to me about this one . . . Oh! . . . has been in the ward so we *have* got the birth history . . . Oh well, let's have him in.'

The doctor then proceeded to do a thorough developmental assessment before checking who else was currently professionally involved in the case.

Such checking was sometimes counterproductive, for although the doctors assumed continuing responsibility for the case, in practice they were unable sometimes to remember particular cases, got them mixed up and had to question parents to establish what they had said last time they met. Such uncertainty was not confined to doctors. In two consultations it became clear that a mother and a grandmother had no idea who they were seeing, let alone why they were seeing this doctor at all. Both referral and introduction in the clinic had been extremely vague. Thus, checking sometimes revealed the doctor as ill informed, flustered and at a disadvantage when faced with a better informed and organized parent who had gathered a lot of information from diverse sources. Typically such parents either seized the opportunity to display their own expertise, with the doctor ceding them the right to structure the clinic agenda, or, in a minority of cases, retreated to a detached and suspicious demeanour which seemed to indicate that the doctor was yet another ill-informed and ineffectual burden with which the parents had to cope. In such cases, the doctor's inability to cure was matched by their inability to demonstrate an instant command of the complexities of the case (Strong and Davis 1978).

Throughout this period the parents were encouraged by the doctor to indicate their feelings about the child, about their domestic circumstances such as the availability of kin who can help out, their expectations for the child, and their expectations of him. They in turn were continually testing the doctor to gain some idea of the child, the extent of medical responsibility for the child, and the types of treatment that could be mobilized for the child.

Various 'clues' were given to the parents about the doctor's view of the child, of what they were expected to adjust to. For example, the doctor might confirm that the child was 'slow', encountered difficulty in tackling activities that 'normal' children do, or that they had too high hopes for the child, e.g. 'You shouldn't push him', etc. The doctor in turn was subject to questioning from the parents as to the outcome, e.g. 'Will he go to a normal school?', 'Is he going to improve?' etc. It was during this process that the doctor indicated what he was prepared to do for the child and also the parents indicated the areas in which the child caused them difficulty. Some of the parents referred overtly to 'not wanting to give him (the child) up' and continued to present the child in as hopeful a light as possible. Even once bad news was out in the open the doctors drew firm limits to their interest. For example doctors never directly enquired in any great detail into family circumstances, income, or family relationships unless the parent first indicated they wish to discuss it. This occurred very rarely. Opportunities were created by the doctor by asking routinely how the parents were coping. Most parents, except in extreme circumstances, said they were coping. However, the doctor rarely indicated that the parents should think of 'giving the child up'. They were expected to cope, with medical intervention being superseded by some form of special education.

There was a group of children, however, for whom this was a likely outcome. The parents and doctor went through the same testing process as in the previous type, but the results were very different. For these children there was no hope of dramatic improvement, they suffered multiple handicaps of some severity, so that neither normal or special schooling was deemed likely to benefit the child by the medical authorities. It was here that the process of ceding the child, of having the medical label as its master status trait, occurred during repeated clinic attendances. It was in these cases that the parents were encouraged by the doctor progressively to scale down their expectations for the child to what the doctor regarded as realistic.

For example, in the following extract the parents had on previous occasions not taken up the doctor's implicit question about their ability to cope but are now indicating that they are beginning to reconsider:

(D) 'How has she been?'

(M) 'Oh, much worse since she's been at home.' (The child had been in care while they were on holiday) 'We are having to feed her now ourselves. It's very difficult.'

(D) 'And what about her sleep? Is she sleeping now?

(F) 'No. She didn't get any sleep last night.'

(D) 'Is she more difficult to handle now?'

(M) 'Yes, she's very much more difficult. The *nurses* said it took two of them to bath her. I mean, how can anyone cope with her? The main problem we have been having is with her feeding. You get very frustrated when you can't do it and you end by smacking her ... '

(Mother goes on to say that she has smacked the child before, that she can understand why children are battered, that she is angry and frightened about what she will do to the child)

(D) 'Yes, I understand. I understand how you can feel like that.'

(They go on to discuss possibilities of some residential care)

The parents who adjusted expectations were regarded as 'good parents', the ones who did not became the subject of case conferences or social work intervention. The doctor continually asked what they thought about the child. He confirmed their doubts and indicated either directly or indirectly (e.g. through offers of periodic in-patient stays) that the child was a candidate for a mental subnormality hospital or severely impaired section of a hospital. The parents usually evidenced considerable distress over this, expressing feelings of guilt, shame, and inadequacy in face of a child who is a 'stranger' to them, and particularly stressed their feelings that it was a sign of bad parenthood to give up their child to some form of residential care (Voysey 1975). Once they had expressed this, the doctor offered them an 'account' for this, legitimating the transfer of responsibility to a medical authority (Scott and Lyman 1968). Parents were told that their 'decision' was 'right', 'best for him' and had honoured any accounts they themselves offered in terms of 'the facilities are better', 'he will be happier there', 'needs specialized nursing', etc. The 'grounds' for the transfer, then, were usually medical ones although other factors were regarded by the doctor as reasonable, e.g. when in one case the unmarried mother of a severely handicapped boy was exploring the possibility of residential care, the doctor honoured this as the mother was working and likely to move out of the district and, also, was likely to marry if the child was suitably placed. In another, the grounds that the mother's health was seriously suffering were sufficient.

Short stays in hospital to allow families to take holidays, and day-care were offered 'to help the parents get used to the idea'. The doctors were however wary about this in case the hospital got used as a place to get rid of such children. Parents were expected to bear the strain as long as possible. In the research we did not see any cases where parents attempted to transfer their children without the context having been well prepared by the doctor before.

The assessment of the child's responsibility was another way in which the ground was prepared in such cases. In the short illness episode cases the issue of responsibility of the child for his actions rarely came up. It was assumed that the child's responsibility was matched by his age in simple terms. The illness was but a short interruption in the process of assuming responsibility. The child's refusal to be 'responsible' however, could in some cases initiate medical consultations. If the child was continually 'wilful', 'high', 'out of control', they were initially referred to the clinics to find out if any underlying medical problem was giving rise to the behaviour. Thus, in one case of suspected epilepsy, the suspicious being rounded in the child's bizarre behaviour, the mother was anxious to know whether the child was ill or not. If it was not, she intended to crack down on the child's behaviour. As she thought the child might be ill, she let the child get away with it. The doctor indicated there was nothing wrong, apart from the 'bad' behaviour that the mother should control before the child did constitute a 'real behaviour problem'.

When the child was disabled or retarded, the issues were less clear-cut. The parents evidence considerable uncertainty as to whether such children were 'really' bad, were responsible, or if the 'badness' was attributable to the diagnosed medical problem (or in two cases to the medication, one of which led to a very irate mother attempting to pin the responsibility on the doctor). The doctor then was forced to pronounce on the moral status of the child. He usually indicated that such children were 'like that', and that they were not to be held responsible for what they do or appear to do. Where the parents did attribute responsibility, the doctor had to convince them otherwise. In one case the mother was worried that her husband typified her severely handicapped girl as both 'wilful' and 'disobedient'. The doctor had previously explained to the mother that although the child was four years old, she was 'really' only nine months old, and therefore not responsible. He decided to talk to the father to attempt to get him to re-define the child. Another mother was alarmed that potty training had failed and said that the child was 'naughty' and 'a nuisance'. The doctor again said that there was no point in pushing the child when it couldn't be expected to perform tasks that other children of similar age took for granted.

Involved in this is an attempt to separate the child's chronological age from its 'real' age in the parents' eyes, to convince them that age-related expectations were invalid in respect of their child. This effectively renders the child 'strange', as one of the basic ways in which we normally interpret others' actions is in terms of chronological age. In separating age from 'real' age, the parents were disbarred from interpreting their child's behaviour in an age-linked developmental sequence. It introduced a sharp discontinuity and made the child unknowable and uninterpretable through the normal everyday procedures for rendering action intelligible. Such a discontinuity served as a further indicator to the parents that something was wrong, and they were consequently forced to adopt the doctor's medical framework to render the child predictable and interpretable. This re-definition of the child as 'not responsible' was an additional indication that severe and continued impairment was likely and that normal expectations were impossible to sustain in such a situation.

Maintaining the relationship

Such medical work as this was believed by the doctors to require a very different kind of doctor, one who eschewed the 'normal' rewards of acute medicine, but instead was prepared to operate in 'grey areas' where 'everything's hazy' and there was no satisfaction through effecting immediate cures by skilled intervention. The work was described by doctors as 'emotionally exhausting' and led to a feeling of impotence in the face of long term, complicated and intractable abnormalities which caused grief and suffering for the parents, which the doctor could do little to alleviate except by listening sympathetically and counselling. Indeed on one case the doctor referred to himself feeling a charlatan for not being able to do much, and in another case said ruefully that 'a man in a fair-ground' would have as much success as he would in predicting the outcome of the child's condition. A small number of parents also alluded to the lack of any point in attendances for them.

It required diplomacy and considerable tactical skills in deploying praise, giving access to resources, persuasion, and the pointing up of possible rewards in order to convince the doubting parents that other services are not as bad as they are commonly portrayed (e.g. the ESN school, the mental subnormality hospital) that all was being done that could be done, and that although fearful, handicap was not so terrible that parents could not cope (Woodmonsey 1971). The role of other services was continually stressed to indicate that parents were not alone, were entitled to and would get appropriate help, even when the doctors at the children's hospital withdrew from the case once the child was in the care of another medical authority.

The inability of the doctor to offer cures for such conditions as spina bifida, cerebral palsy, or mental retardation disrupted the normal pattern of medical services, which was the treatment of specific illness episodes with a determinate outcome terminating the relationship. Cures were in short supply in these clinics and this created a continuing relationship with an indeterminate outcome. In particular, for the parents it raised acutely the problem of just what the consultations were for. The doctor was also aware of this and was forced to offer some grounds for involvement in case the parents found the whole thing pointless and decide to terminate the relationship. A few parents did drop out. The doctor attempted to maintain contact by offering up to three more appointments. If the parents did not turn up, the case was formally returned to the GP.

The parents initially expected the doctor to produce a cure or at least some improvement through the manipulation of medical knowledge — whereas the doctor often had little idea of the causes and prognosis of the problem, let alone of effective treatment. At the first meeting, however, only the boldest of the parents asked direct questions about this, e.g. 'Is there anything that can be done for him?', 'Can you do anything to bring him on?', 'Is he going to walk?', and the doctor could therefore usually get away with fairly vague statements — 'He's a bit behind, we'll have to wait and see'. This was usually justified by the doctor on the ground of (a) a genuine indeterminacy in diagnosis and prognosis; (b) the necessity of breaking such bad news gently, but it also serves their purpose of building and maintaining a relationship (Davis 1966).

However, after two or three such meetings, most parents would appear to demand direct answers and for the doctor this constituted the crisis point in the relationship, as he had then to explain what could be done for such children. He quite explicitly referred to the lack of cures but added that marginal alleviation of the child's disabilities could be achieved through the provision of specialist therapy and equipment, e.g. physiotherapy may improve the child's balance and co-ordination; braces and splints may allow the child to become more mobile; drugs may control a child's behaviour if it is too gross; speech therapy may improve the child's verbal skills, etc.

Since diagnosis and prognosis were tentatively phrased, the doctors could offer the possible validation of 'improvement' at repeat visits or at least greater certainty. Similarly, through his knowledge of the system of care he was able to offer the parents his services in eliciting help from various supportive services and organizations, or help the parents get such benefits as attendance allowances, grants for special equipment; check out any complaints they have about other medical or para-medical services, etc. He also offered limited counselling services, discussing the family's domestic problems, e.g. housing and transport problems, or coping with the family's worries about the child. The doctors sometimes offered minor medical treatment; during their routine medical examination of the child they often noticed rashes, etc. and recommended appropriate treatment.

Thus, as the doctor could not usually offer cures, he attempted to assume the role of co-ordinator or 'manager' for the child in relation to the various specialized services that cater for disabled children.

All these were inducements for the parents to remain in the relationship, even though their typification of the doctor as someone who cures had to be abandoned. The parents learnt to change their demands for cures into requests for physiotherapy, help in supporting applications for equipment, money, housing changes, etc. This task was somewhat limited in so far as the doctors were not in a position to mobilize all these various services to order. They were not in control of the other medical specialisms in the hospital, nor were they in charge of admissions procedures to various institutions and services which are run by the Local Authority health, statutory, and voluntary social work organizations. Thus, the role they assumed was a difficult one, its credibility was always under attack. They were subject to the exigencies of waiting lists and the decision-making process of other organizations which may take their recommendations into account, but did not recognize their right to make any decision on the parents' entitlement. Where parents continue to make such demands they were forced into a collaborative strategy with them, discussing tactics, etc. but unable to assure a particular outcome.

Similarly, this 'role' overlaps with those of other professionals, e.g. 'counselling' may constitute interference with the social workers, while the treatment of the child's minor illnesses might be the prerogative of the GP so that the case has to be referred back to him, though they may recommend a particular course of treatment.

Thus, in one sense the doctor's task became a holding operation until some final outcome was negotiated either within a medical setting, e.g. residential care, or was resolved by the educational authority when they decided on the appropriate schooling for the child at age five. Thus, some of the consultations had little which is explicitly 'medical' in content, in fact it sometimes seemed that both the doctor and parents had some difficulty in finding something to talk about if little had occured since the last visit. The time was filled in with the routine testing, a few questions about other services, and the doctor flicking through the case notes in search of new topics of conversation or things to check. Some parents, therefore, particularly working-class ones, seem to define repeated visits as a waste of time and ceased coming.

Even for those who stayed, a mutual accommodation with the doctor was not always possible. A further condition for this is some agreed-upon definition of the child's problem and the prognosis, and some parents persisted for many years in holding hidden definitions that were widely discrepant with the doctors, e.g. one spastic child had been having piano lessons to improve his co-ordination and his parents then envisaged a career as a music teacher for him. In such cases each meeting with the parents was extremely difficult for the doctor since he had to attempt once again to convince them of his diagnosis. Others (very few) may have had their hopes revived by another form of treatment, such as Doman-Delcato, or through seeing or reading about a disease that resembled their child's symptoms had rejected the doctor's version in favour of one that appeared to offer them hope or greater therapeutic potential, such as 'autism'.

However, parents who accepted the diagnosis and who got some reward at least from their repeated visits became 'old hands'. They knew what the doctor was interested in, what sorts of information he required, what his questions meant and what sorts of things he could and could not do for the child. Similarly the doctor knew the parents, had judged their reliability, worked out what was at stake for them with the child, the likely outcome of the case, and so on. The doctor offered parents some 'medical'/'therapeutic' role that they could 'share' with him. They could become an assistant, observing the behaviour he himself could not witness, interpreting that which he could not understand, aiding him in his testing of the patient. As such he was then able to check out his opinions with them, offer them friendly advice, suggest joint strategies, e.g. 'I think *we* should ...' Both sets of participants may then have something to offer each other which the other values or had learnt to value. It may not perhaps be very much, but in this difficult situation it may be the best that is available.

In this chapter we have tried to show the ways in which the transition from a normal to a handicapped identity is managed. Rather than there being some single point at which the parents were notified that things have changed for the worse, it has been emphasized that there are a whole number of features of the work done and its setting as the last specialist referral in the system that together created a context of doubt and ambiguity around the child's identity. The clinic typically dealt with cases which could ultimately be recruited to a permanent spoiled identity. The ways in which this recruitment was done, i.e. by creating a childhood that was a set of parental tasks requiring special advice in handling and management, by changing expectations and treating their child as different, special, and strange, was a gradual and uneasy process. The message was communicated in diverse ways; tacitly by continually breaching normal assumptions about childhood, by detailed questioning of parents, by repeated checking, testing, and dismantling of children's competencies; the separation of 'real' and 'chronological' age; the maintenance of uncertainty, recalls, and refusal to marvel. These all worked to produce uncertainty and ambiguity and serious doubt. Overtly, parental claims were doubted, bad news was broken, medicine's ineffectuality was stressed, 'management' was substituted for cure, and *shared* responsibility indicated. Taken together these constitute a powerful doubt inducing and indentity reinforcing status, particularly when backed by hospital specialist authority.

The passage was further eased by a number of structural factors. It was isolated, there was no group going through the same experience. Indeed some parents feared contamination of their children by their sharing facilities with more severely handicapped children. At the current state of medical knowledge there was no physically alternative passage available, i.e. no cures. The clinic itself offered some help in managing the irrevocable physical deterioration of cerebral palsy, etc., if the fact of the status passage was accepted by the parents.

7

Separate worlds:
Children as work

So far we have described settings in which children and their parents were co-present and have tried to show the ways in which tensions between the social and clinical worlds manifested themselves as dilemmas for the doctors, and the manner in which these dilemmas were resolved in practice. In doing so we have distinguished two main modes of medical work, initiative and receptive and described different features of the work settings which influence the performance of medical work. In order to push the point home a little harder we shall now consider another form of medical work which was marked by the *absence* of a parental audience, where children were treated apart from their mothers, namely a special nursery attached to a maternity unit and physiotherapy and occupational therapy. We noted earlier on that medical work has to pay some attention to social matters (however minimal) if only because the object of medical treatment is itself social. The two settings we shall discuss in this chapter were segregated, in that continual parental involvement was neither sought nor thought a desirable objective.

Given that the person treated was a young child, their as yet asocial character allowed social courtesies to be superseded by purely technical and professional concerns. Such settings' professional participants worked with a shared knowledge of a corpus of medical knowledge. This engineering model was segregated from parental surveillance for a number of reasons which we shall discuss later on (McKeown 1976).

Both settings were characterized by a collegial structure differentiated by skill and formal position. Peer surveillance was a characteristic of both settings; one ward round consisted of ten or more doctors and nurses, while therapy was done in front of at least one other therapist. Both were preoccupied with technical aspects of medicine, though as we shall see, the issues of children's and parent's cooperation had greater salience for therapy than in the nursery, where such liaison work had the same problematic features as we described in the last chapter in the section on 'Telling', except that it was telling at one remove.

Strategic, narrow technical concerns were overt amongst the staff in both departments, a feature noticeably absent from work done in front of parents. Similarly, professional concerns were also legitimate topics of conversation, again a feature noticeably absent from work done in front of parents. Mistakes at work were openly acknowledged and scientific or technical virtuosity were rewarded by peers. Cases were interesting or not interesting, but their interest lay not in their social features but in the technical sophistication and medical interest that they exemplified. In short, children were problematic objects to which technical solutions were required. The points at which those technical solutions were contingent on parents were ones of tension, but due to segregation of the technical world from the parental world such points were limited in number and in scope.

The special nursery

The special nursery was in some ways unique. It was the one setting along with the maternity hospital that generated basic medical records on children. The work that was performed in the nursery had widespread organizational implications. Just to have been in the nursery automatically generated a request to parents to attend the follow-up clinic for screening. Birth data and data on neonatal illness or injury were routinely required by other medical services for children to enable them to construct a medical biography as an aid to diagnosis. Thus, special discharge notes were routinely sent to the Local Authority Health Department and to GPs, and were also lodged in the child's own hospital medical record. To have been in the nursery was indicative of authoritative medical doubt, in some degree, about the health status of the child. Precisely because the nursery generated this doubt it was resolved by follow-up screening of the type we have discussed.

The wideness of admission criteria had implications beyond technical ones. Given the large number of possible variables associated with handicap and retardation, admission to the nursery implied that some aspect of the child was 'abnormal' enough to require separation of mother and child, and placement of the child in a 'special' nursery with a high staff-patient ratio. Staff, not surprisingly, attributed the high turn-up rate for subsequent screening to the anxiety that this separation induced in the mother. But as we have already seen as the criteria for admission were wide there was little pathology to be found in the population follow-up. While the appropriateness of wide criteria was the subject of considerable discussion by the nursery staff, their provisional medical nature was never mentioned to parents in our hearing. Staff might doubt the appropriateness of the criteria but once admitted a child ineluctably collected a record that invoked screening, notification of the Local Authority Health Department, notification of the GP, hospital record, and inclusion of the child on the Local Authority 'at risk' list. Doctors recognized the shortcomings of this inclusiveness (a large follow-up population and much anxiety) but nevertheless maintained a liberal policy. Nursery rounds further served to provide daily affirmation of the policy as each new arrival was inspected to see whether its admission was justified (Arluke 1980).

For example,

> 'A "new" case was presented as having been admitted due to "concern downstairs" (maternity hospital). On inspection the child was "a good colour" and "looks well". The junior doctor who admitted the child said: "I'm treating this as a normal baby". Others on round agree that child should go back on the wards soon. Child is then taken out of incubator and put in a cot.'

Just as other parts of the network received trade unpredictably as a consequence of others decisions, so too did the nursery, as its trade was determined by individual doctors' decision after childrens delivery in the maternity hospital. But collegial, visible inspection of such decisions served to rule out and check purely idiosyncratic decision-making. It consequently became an arena not only for immediate interventionist discussions but also for discussion for the relationship of the nursery with other medical services, usually in the context of particular cases. For example, discussions of the impossibility of constructing check-lists of tests as some days 'bloods' were not available, or how difficult it was to get X-rays done if the maternity hospital machine was not working occurred routinely.

These comments on current 'policy' and working arrangements with other services were again topics never discussed in front of parents except where the doctor was seeking referral. Critical remarks were rarely made of other services by doctors though they were by parents. But as the nursery's work often involved other specialists and services, current relationships were openly discussed. Thus, what was going on in the maternity wards, the other services' work-loads and the availability of diagnostic tests, relations with general and orthopaedic surgeons, were discussed openly and sometimes critically. A long critical discussion on one round was concerned with the surest means that could be used to find a particularly elusive specialist.

While the nursery provided cots, nursing, and medical supervision, other medical specialties were invoked for particular cases. Who was doing what to whom and when and how was routinely checked on the daily ward round. Such discussion could also be at a level of personal knowledge of character and competence, again issues never discussed in front of parents except to point up the skilled and competent nature of the work the parents were or would be getting.

Further, wider professional concerns were also issues of legitimate discussion. For example, the question of why the nursery was having so many children requiring exchange transfusions in the past two months was raised as an issue and discussed at length. Again, this was rarely, if ever, manifested to out-patient clinics. The doctors displayed an interest in medicine, in professional paraphernalia, in quoting journals, research reports and their findings, other research in progress elsewhere, ethics, new developments and also in publishing articles on children with new or unusual medical conditions (Duff and Campbell 1973). As the doctors also had teaching posts, children in the nursery were also candidates for providing teaching material through photographs, slides, or tape recordings.

It is in such settings as these that much medical work is performed. This would seem to offer some evidence for collegial control albeit of an indirect kind. For in all such settings implicit evaluation was carried on, and was presumably known to be carried on by other doctors. Such knowledge might well have some impact on actual medical practice (others will inspect your work and your 'reputation' will be established) and lead to doctors looking over their shoulders. Even GPs were monitorable to a degree through their hospital referral practices in the NHS, as we have seen in Chapter 5.

Such collegial setting also encouraged a provisional approach to medical intervention. Treatment was discussed as uncertain and unpredictable in its outcome in a detail that never occurred in an out-patient clinic, except when parents were out of the room, and sometimes not even then. Thus one long interchange on a ward round concerned the differing bilirubin levels at which exchange transfusions are generally done; the consultant ended it with an admonition to 'be flexible' but established that he preferred a particular benchmark for transfusion although other specialists differed in their policy.

Mistakes were acknowledged without overt censure and demonstration of diagnostic acumen rewarded with praise. It might be argued that such mistakes should be censured. It appeared that if doctors worked with an assumption that mistakes will occur (like in aeroplane crashes or mining disasters) it was more important to have collegial knowledge of such potential disasters in order to prevent them in the future (e.g. by instituting further equipment sterility checks). Public censure, like the possibility of litigation, was more likely to lead to concealment, or defensive medicine.

In a setting where parental concerns were absent or distant features, the doctors had a version of childhood that was overtly scientific. The children (neonates) were in no position to interfere, their co-operation was not required in treatment, and the parents were absent. All these features allowed a view of children as technical problems rather than social beings. Thus it was rare for children to be marvelled at or to be singled out as desirable objects. Instead, they were work. While in interview doctors made much of how different paediatrics was from normal medicine or that both mother and child were the treatment unit, it was interesting to note that in the absence of the mother and with a new baby, paediatric practice conformed closely to a clinical format which others have described (Goffman 1961: 115-32.)

The technical problems that children presented were of differing degree ranging from mild jaundice to severe illness. While the former type required only routine medical recipes such as phototherapy or surveillance to ensure consistent weight gain, the ones that were singled out for most attention were the 'puzzles' and the 'exotic'. Thus on the ward round minor updating on progress (or lack of it) would suffice to check on most of the children, but others would become the focus of great attention and interest because of the diagnostic or treatment difficulties they presented. However, once other specialisms were treating the child then the child would be regarded as an interesting case but without the nursery concern. The major concern with such children was that the nursery was adequately performing in its own restricted way of feeding and maintenance. In such cases an uneasy relationship with other services existed over rights in the child; whether for example nursery routines should be broken when another specialist 'suddenly' required a child, e.g. for surgery.

While in other clinics we noted how addressing the child was a way of conveying normality, in this setting children could not be used to convey messages to parents. Such messages had to be more direct. Mothers were allowed to 'visit' their children in the nursery but terms of access were set by the medical staff and indeed admission to the nursery was guarded by a doorbell symbolically marking it off as a separate and non-permeable setting. Such separation and 'visiting' were acknowledged to cause anxiety, but doctors portrayed this as functional, for it raised motivation to attend follow-up. The obvious array of technology in the setting and restricted access served to create parental doubt about the child.

In such a sealed setting with its own concerns, bridging the clinical world and the parental world created problems. This was a constant preoccupation of the nursing staff who always sought a definite time for discharge that they could tell mothers, or asked 'What should the mother be told?', presumably because they were most likely to be asked. Bridging was also done by the senior doctor when there was serious illness to be disclosed or a condition that might 'shock' parents. Difficult and emotionally charged communications were taken as part of the consultant's duty. Attempts were made to ensure some continuity of contact by rotating staff through other parts of the paediatric network so that they would be likely to see the child and mother again. In practice we were informed that this did not in fact work, because of the necessity of constantly redeploying staff according to the demands of the hospital's paediatric clinics as a whole.

The mother's reliability or identity was rarely an issue (in fact it was not necessary to know some babies' names). Treatment did not depend on such prior identification. The mothers were only discussed on rounds when they were a source of trouble to the performance of clinical medicine e.g. when parents were Jehovah's witnesses, or where very bad news had to be broken, where the child looked illshaped and alarming, where the wrong prognosis might have been given, or where the mother was not able to 'visit' the child because of her own illness.

On the rare occasions when children were admired or dandled they were invariably children ready to go back on the wards. Admiration in this medical frame indicated medical success, a source of collective praise for good medical intervention and good news for the parents. This was rare though — most children were work. Indeed, praise and marvelling was only ever done by the nurses if it was done at all.

We shall turn to the other setting which was segregated from parental involvement. We shall see that in the case of the therapies that tactical considerations and parental cooperation were at a premium.

Therapy: children as work

The therapies were in a similar position to the 'receptive' settings, responding to demands made by doctors for their services. However, there was an important difference between physiotherapy and occupational therapy — the former being long-established and the latter relatively new in the hospital. Referral routes for physiotherapy were well established and the therapists able to exert considerable control over what cases they were referred. The occupational therapists had no secure 'trade' and sought to create it by holding open days, giving lots of feedback to doctors, and so on (Rushing 1964). While unable to discharge a child without medical warrant or to treat without one, the enclosed settings they worked in meant that within referred 'trade' they could and did allocate time as they deemed necessary.

Thus, some cases could be treated thoroughly, and others lightly supervised depending on the current volume of trade. Also, as therapists set their own recall policy, it was possible to schedule work in a manner that suited them, putting cases on morning or afternoon, daily, weekly, fortnightly, or monthly recall depending on what they wanted or felt they could achieve. Ward work, on the other hand, was out of their control and again depended on decisions made elsewhere. It had to be done twice or three times daily, and also for 'cover', therapists were on call over weekends for urgent ward work such as chest drainage for a child seriously ill with pneumonia.

Unlike the other types of medical work described so far, therapy with young children who are abnormal in some way demands a much closer involvement with the child and a lesser involvement with the parents. Whereas in the other setting the child was there to be examined or tested, this constituted the limits of medical attention given to him. In therapy the child became the main target of work for the duration of the treatment session. While other doctors had strategic concerns about managing smooth interaction with children so as to get through the encounter in good order, when treatment was undertaken such strategic concerns are heightened. The main reason for this was the nature of childhood itself. We have already referred to the ways in which the sick-role formulation fails to encompass those who cannot understand the obligations it entails. In face of this incompetence the strategic problems of treatment, if it is to be done at all, had to be solved by the therapist. These strategic problems remain no matter what the therapeutic purpose might be.

Six types of tasks can be distinguished based on the allocative decisions of the therapists.

GENERAL PREVENTIVE AND CORRECTIVE WORK

Here the objective was either to prevent malfunctioning occurring through early intervention to correct limb functions or postural defects through exercises and stimulation.

SPECIFIC COMPETENCES

Here the objective is to develop some very specific competences or to treat a localized medical problem, e.g. pre-operative chest drainage, leg exercises for immobilised children on the wards. Such work was normally in the form of routine requests for treatment of children on one ward and lasted usually only for the duration of their hospital stay.

RECONSTRUCTION

Here children lack very basic motor or intellectual competences. The object was either to restore these functions or to develop motor competences to the child's limits. The whole child was the object of therapy and such cases were typically long-term ones.

SOCIAL SUPPORT

This included such social objectives as providing some service in 'hopeless' cases by taking the child off the mothers' hands for a while, by giving parents advice on clothing, stimulation, recipes for daily living, special equipment, and so on.

TIME OUT

Such cases were typically short-term visits to therapy for children on the wards to provide them with something to do.

STIMULATION

This was rather a vague category but referred to those children for whom the therapeutic purpose was to enrich their cognitive environment by purposeful stimulation.

Within each task there were different modes of involvement

which were employed by therapists. Here we can distinguish four different types of involvement which are typically associated with the different types of cases.

THE CLINICAL MODE

Here children were treated as clinical objects. Clinical comments were made about them during treatment in their 'hearing'. Such children had been closely inspected for signs of normal competences and had been found wanting, e.g. the profoundly retarded or spastic children. Age was no barrier to the use of the clinical mode for chronological age was irrelevant in denoting the level of child development. Rather, their basic deficiency was a master trait that obliterated all else except when parents were present. Only then were they treated as social, but it was a 'polite fiction' rather than an accurate descrition. Such children were used overtly as teaching material for student therapists and prognoses given out in front of the child not matter how grim or discrediting. Any other form of involvement was deemed impossible, and if attempted, discredited as irrelevant. Such cases were worthy of pity and great sadness as little could be done for them other than maintaining supple limbs through passive exercises. The therapist had to do all the work, the child could not 'help' and was not expect to.

TECHNICAL

Where the therapeutic purpose was very specific or dependent upon or subordinate to other medical work done elsewhere the mode of involvement was a technical one. No long term relationship was either likely or therapeutically desirable. The children making up this category posed technical problems, e.g. limb mobilization, but apart from this problem the therapist had no reason to seek any other involvement with what was likely to be a short term case. Such cases were usually serviced on the wards. Thus, therapists were friendly enough with such children but not committed to them. They may cause problems, e.g. in producing breathing exercises, but such problems were resolved easily enough by the recipes described elsewhere (Davis and Strong 1975). Typically such children were 'normal' apart from some temporary defect such as a broken limb, and were usually able to understand the point of therapy. They were not touched or handled as much as other children but rather instructed to perform exercises. Thus, the death of one such child on the ward with severe pneumonia was made memorable to the therapists not least because of the technical problems involved in treating such a very sick child, as well as the tragedy of the death itself.

INVOLVED

This typically occurred in long-term therapeutic relationships where the therapist was involved in displaying a number of different identities to the child, as tutor, friend, and playmate, as well as therapist and adult. These were all possible in long-term relationships, particularly the reconstruction cases where the therapist and child developed a warmer and more intimate relationship. However, it was precisely in these kinds of relationships that strategic considerations were at a premium for they required not only involvement from the therapist but involvement from the child as well. Where the child was old enough to understand the objective, e.g. at ages five and six and upwards, this was less of a problem than with younger ones. In such cases co-operation became a major problem to be solved if anything was to be achieved at all. As we have argued elsewhere the typical resolution of these problems was to adopt a framework within which the therapeutic activities could be seen as 'play', although this framework generated its own problems (Davis and Strong 1975).

UNINVOLVED

In some cases the relationship was a very attenuated one, for example where older children were attending for 'sunlights' (phototherapy) all that needed doing was to set up the apparatus and leave the child to it. Similarly, children without therapeutic potential who were foisted onto therapists for other reasons than specific therapeutic purposes were 'held' under light supervision but little involvement. Such children typically constructed their own agendas, games, and toys for 'time out' or 'social support' cases.

These then were the major modes or relationship between the therapists and their charges. But as we noted earlier the 'involved' relationship was a hazardous one to construct because of the need for co-operation from the child. Creating such a relationship depended on the therapists' ability continually to create the involvement necessary for therapeutic success. To do this a number tactics were adopted, one of which was the game framework tioned earlier. These could be grouped under the following : attention getting, sanctioning, dependency creation, and self-ness.

Attention-getting was done in a number of ways. Conversation was monopolized by the therapist talking to the child all the time, but to no-one else in the room, a constant barrage of talk designed to restrict the possibilities of outside involvements. Where 'distractions' did occur these too were turned into talk between therapist and child. Thus verbally the child's attention was turned continually to the tasks at hand by describing them, questioning the child about them, and commenting on performance of them. The talk invariably contained a competitive structure, to set the child tasks and to talk to him as he 'competed' to attain these targets so that he tested himself to the limits. Such targets could be used as inducements — 'Three more and we'll do something else' — setting the number and duration of tasks, promising a change to something else once the task has been completed.

Such attention-getting tactics were reinforced by the way they were also attention-giving, demonstrating interest, enjoyment, fun, and committment to the exclusivity of the relationship by the therapist. Everything the child did on the mat was of interest to the therapist and the exclusiveness of the attention given precluded any escape by the child. The whole child was relevant and routines were established and policed by sanctioning as well as play.

The issue of who was in control intermittently came to the fore over issues of routine switching, general rebelliousness, or improper orientation to tasks and routines. When children refused to perform as desired the range of *sanctions* was, in fact, limited. While mothers may smack their children it was not deemed professional for a therapist to smack a recalcitrant child. However there were some other possibilities available, the ones normally available to all adults, threats, bribes, sharpness of tone. Therapists deliberately refused to give in and switch treatment routines, to indicate that tears do not end a treatment session, and that it has to go on despite the breakdown of one session or one routine. Therapists resorted to threats of sterner measures, switches to passive movements, refusal to change to pleasanter activities or allow the child to withdraw or escape, and sometimes ridicule.

The potential for sanctioning was created by the mother's absence. Therapists insisted on mothers not being present, not just because they created problems as audiences but because their absence gave them total control over the *dependent* child. Mothers could not be appealed to, to retrieve the child from an unhappy situation. Their absence allowed the therapist to take over a set of adult rewards that normally parents would allocate, cuddling the child, kindly chat and enthusiasm for the child's fads, helping the child enjoy the toys available in the room, playing, and so on, as well as more mundane motherly activities like dressing children, wiping noses, and cleaning up vomit or faeces.

A further tactic concerned the development of the child's *self-consciousness*. As children cannot immediately see the point of therapy they can at least 'feel' what they are doing. Reference was continually made to the child's sensations by the therapists, spelling out what she should experience in moving her own body. The objective of this was eventually to get the child to monitor herself in a self-conscious way. Thus, children became aware of muscles, arm positions, walking gait, through the therapists' constant attention to them and progressively were able to take responsibility to correct the disability themselves. To begin with, it was not of course a conscious process on the child's part, but continual and specific attention to a leg muscle or arm position (like nail-biting) makes the child 'aware' of its anatomy in a way that others are not unless they are involved in some deliberate physical activity like athletes.

Once the child became aware of having a physical problem and of the steps taken to overcome it then treatment did not have to be so heavily controlled by the therapist. Rather, the therapist could become a willing audience to feats of endurance and heroism as children's set tasks were self-consciously bettered or new targets set by the child himself, e.g.

> (T) 'Come on — ten press-ups — I'll count.'
> (C) 'I can do thirty!'
> (T) 'Can you? All right, then, off you go.'
> (T counts, child collapses at 20)
> (T) 'That's marvellous. Well done.'

Once this stage had been reached such children ceased to be hard work, but could be relied upon to swing from routine to routine like practiced music hall artists.The therapist as audience only had to applaud and occasionally intervene.

While such intimate relationships have therapeutic utility, they also have their dangers. Familiarity could and did breed contempt unless controlled. While children seemed to view their therapists with affection, e.g. using nick names developed through the relationship, the therapist's involvement was rather more ambivalent. While much may be achieved by involvement it must remain *tactical* involvement. One child with winning ways was in r of becoming the 'pet' of a particular therapist with a uent ceding of control over therapy sessions to the child. dangers were averted by strong collegial control over the t, the child, once out of control, being given to another therapist for 'the big stick' treatment as it was called. Of course, once such a relationship had been created the very threat of its unilateral removal could provide the necessary disciplinary measures. The tactical nature of the relationship was also reinforced by therapists also having to treat children they had grown to dislike. Children could be penances as well as rewards.

Unless the relationship was developed early on in the child's treatment therapy became a continuous battleground. Some, the profoundly retarded, never did have the competences for such a relationship to develop. One or two others vitiated the relationship by being literally out of control. One case in particular caused continual problems as *none* of the available tactics worked. A constant preoccupation of the therapist concerned was whether the child was mentally disturbed or merely very clever, having discovered the limits of the therapist's authority. The child routinely swore at her, bit her, hit her, cried, and destroyed others' sessions by disrupting the exclusiveness of the relationship. There was little the therapist could do. Other children caused local difficulties, acting up, taking sneaky short-cuts in therapy, refusing to comply, and 'trying it on' by claiming tiredness or illness. Normal control recipes usually worked with such children and their disruptiveness could be a source of amusement, precisely because they took place within an established framework in which the therapist has had ample opportunity to assess the child's character. Thus, when one five-year-old hemiplegic claimed to be tired and then started coughing pathetically at one end of the mat, this was not regarded with much sympathy but with humour and mild ridicule until eventually he was told to 'stop faking it — I know you of old — you can come off it — come on — crawl back to me — can't you? You must be getting old.'

To assess children's character proved easier over a longer period and it did not matter so much over a short one — nobody knew what most of the ward cases were like as children. Some ward cases were memorable, an embarrassing 'screamer' in particular who shrieked hysterically throughout the session much to the embarrassment of the therapist, alarm of other children, and amusement of the nurses. Mostly they were not. Of those treated in the therapy rooms only some were 'memorable'. They formed 'archetypes' (like 'tragedies'), special cases that bore retelling because they exemplified therapeutic points. One rarely found general rules spelt out in therapy except in very technical discussion — rather more common were detailed *social* and characterological histories of striking families or children that differentiated 'the CP children' or 'the spina bifidas' or 'the hemis'.

In long term cases — 'character' had to be assessed to work out how best to 'approach children', e.g. ignore, compete, play, instruct, as different tactics worked better with different children. In reaching such conclusions about children it was recognized that a correct assessment could not really be made until some treatment pre-conditions had been established. New cases needed several sessions to become 'happy' and 'under control', and the first few sessions were written off as 'play' or 'a lot of crying and shouting'. Thus, a lot of time was spent chatting up children and getting children's confidence before treatment and assessment could proceed.

It was also recognized that children displayed behaviour that was different from normal clinic out-patient behaviour in the therapy room. This sometimes provides a source of information denied to others. One small girl's fortuitous chatting to another small boy provided grounds for the therapist's belief that the child was not as backward as the doctor in charge thought — the child talked spontaneously and was not 'parroting' and was 'sociable' despite a low formal IQ score. (Sometimes therapists wished doctors could see children under such spontaneous conditions — rather like the ideal expressed in integrated assessment units for children.) On the other hand it was difficult to tell what some children were like. When there was no recognizable feedback from children it was difficult to tell what was going on in children's minds despite a lot of contact — some children defied any interpretation.

In typing children therapists did not go in for marvelling — they did not have to — it was not necessary as there was no parental audience. Children were 'work', but also interesting, amusing, and fun to work with as well as nasty, mucky, messy, vicious, spiteful, dirty, etc. Many children were seen over a period of years, and experience dulled the natural production of wonder — 'work' took over and children were viewed through this set of lenses. Children's character could be all the above adjectives but revealed as such by *work*. Similarly, the *work* accomplished depended on what the child was like, easy-going, hard, stubborn, etc.

Only by long contact could therapists learn to 'read' children correctly; furthermore, children could fool therapists so all characteristizations were provisional. Other traps awaited the unwary. Mothers were regarded routinely as bad story-tellers and clinics were regarded as bad places to get 'real' information on children. Nevertheless, the medical notes were used to fill in gaps in therapists' knowledge, e.g. what the child's IQ was.

There were many other ways to get information on children — as the relationship was ongoing it was possible to assess the mental and social elements affecting performance and improvements (if any), any tiredness or back-sliding. Tiredness was assessed by appearance, by the relation of effort to actual performance, and knowledge of the child's daily routines. Mental abilities were assessed in the course of therapy, utilizing activities such as drawing, naming colours, describing, giving commands, all of which gave the therapist necessary information on what could be mobilized successfully for work. Parents were also evaluated via their children, for example, checking when children go to bed by asking which TV programmes they watched. Over time they could assess if original impressions were correct, e.g.:

(Therapist A) 'There's more to that child than meets the
                eye!'
(because C chatters)
(Therapist B) 'Oh, I didn't know she could talk!'

(And later on, doing crawling exercises by command)

(Therapist A) 'Oh, I don't suppose you know left and right!'

Overt liveliness was but one indicator of normality — but one 'lively' child turned out to have an IQ of 30!

Assessing the parents was also necessary. A continual therapist's problem was the relationship between what goes on at home and what goes on in therapy. Ideally parents should turn up on time, their children fresh and clean having had supportive treatment at home. On the other hand parents deviate from the ideal by encouraging 'bad' habits, choosing shoes for cosmetic rather than therapeutic reasons, under-stimulating and over-feeding the child, and worst of all, giving the child laxatives before therapy. All these created problems for the therapist.

However, while these may be problems they were never directly addressed, for to do so could cause defaulting or complaints. Even here where therapy was held to be undermined by an 'odd' background, the background might be cause for inter-professional disputes but not overt attacks on the parent. Instead, therapists worked to 'attach' the parents to the team by offering sympathy and a promise of improvement. Reports on current therapeutic progress were routinely given, though never prognoses or even diagnoses, these were squarely in the doctor's domain. Consequently, parents were encouraged to drop in to see therapists, to chat to them about their problems and received sympathy, consideration and, where possible, practice help or advice in return. Any attempts to 'pump' the therapist to check on the doctor were firmly resisted. Such medical information as was given out was limited in its scope to the task of therapy and never strayed beyond it.

As we noted, parents were absent during these encounters. The mother deposited the child and came to the therapy room to collect the child at the end of the therapy session. Invariably collecting the child coincided with the final set of exercises, often the 'high' point of the session such as aided walking. This accomplishment invariably provided a useful topic for bridging the clinical and social world, the mother could admire the child's progress, while the therapist could demonstrate what could be achieved with further parental co-operation.

The limits to the information that therapists would give were quite clear. If advice on shoes, exercise, home management, etc. was required then it was freely given to help mobilize the parents toward valid therapeutic objectives. But when for example a mother displayed an incorrect, over-optimistic typification of the child, that was something that required medical authority for it involved giving a prognosis. Such parental errors were reported to the doctor concerned as a right, but were never directly addressed by the therapist who would typically leave the issue open ended: 'Well — let's wait and see, shall we?'. Such 'errors' formed part of the folklore of therapy, a constant reminder to be on guard against giving hostages to fortune, and about upsetting both the mother and doctor.

What we have tried to do in this section is to show that segregative medicine 'solves' a number of dilemmas that are present in out-patients encounters. The medical model can be safely emphasized and a shared clinical orientation can be assumed in doing the work. The absence of parents means that the only audiences to medical work are other workers and a child who cannot intervene much to impede treatment. The mode of involvement does not have to give deference to the social nature of the encounter or to the primary role of the parent as guardian of the child. Instead clinical concerns can supersede social ones. 'Telling' occurs at the end of the encounter and interaction with parents is minimal or supportive. Teaching can be safely done without fear of information leaking out that might disrupt or disturb the relationship between worker and patient. Similarly, the clinical identities of the children are insulated from other social identities. The degree of doubt about the child is considerable in the nursery and is seen as functional for relationship maintenance while in therapy the issue of normality or abnormality is either out in the open and shared by parent and therapist or if in 'error' a responsibility for the doctor to rectify, not the therapist.

Thus, detachment, technical identities, and a strategic concern were foremost in segregative medicine.

8

The Medical Management
of Identity

We have noted that the years from birth to five years old are characterized by many points of contact between medical services and children. We have also noted that these contacts are made by a number of different services for different medical purposes, some stemming from medical concern with the child population as a whole, others from contact sought by parents of specific children for specific medical purposes. In both cases the task of the doctor is to adjudicate on the health status of the child, to make a clinical decision whether to admit or exclude the child from further organized health care contact.

However, as Freidson notes, in differentiating the ill from the not ill the doctor is also involved, whether he likes it or not, in offering not just a clinical decision but also a social identity, a way of socially categorizing the child (Freidson 1970). In an earlier section we argued that these identities are not conveyed by words alone but by a whole constellation of factors that make up 'communication'. As well as verbal descriptions or clinical terms, doctors also used demeanour, differential attention, different styles of questioning and history taking, and appeals to normal childhood in an overt fashion, as well as responding to and recreating the more general meanings attached to different parts of the system as a whole. By this I mean that, for example, the 'seriousness' of the special neurological clinic was created in part out of its location in the network of services as a whole, while, say, the relative informality of Local Authority organized screening took its meaning and significance from its concern with total populations rather than with specific illnesses. The criteria for entry to the different settings, their disposition and the way in which their clientele was selected for them served to shape the flow of children so that typically different settings 'offered' different types of identities to their clientele. Each setting received its clientele already shaped by prior medical or organizational decisions in such a way as to ensure its clients were 'typical'. One of the sources of the routine medical work in the different settings was the way in which the individual settings 'trade' was *made* routine by continual medical differentiation of the whole population. This was matched by the inability of the second-line experts to shape their 'trade' except by indirect means or by large-scale organizational readjustment.

It would seem that the system as a whole develops by adding new 'workshops' to deal with clients who do not fit easily into existing arrangements. Once established, workshops referred clients selectively so that their flow of clients became characterized as of a particular kind. Once knowledge of the new workshop and its clientele spreads, its clientele is further stabilized as all cases of a particular type are funnelled through the network towards it and through differentiation decisions being made in other workshops in the system in the light of the 'new' provision. Work will be found for the new workshop in other workshops if only because their own organizational and diagnostic repertoire is expanded by its addition. The special neurological clinic was a good case in point. It was set up because of dissatisfaction with existing organizational arrangements for dealing with long-term handicapped children. Once established, it served as a reference point for other specialists and GPs for cases they could not handle, attracting such cases and eventually becoming known as the appropriate clinic for such cases. Given, as we have argued, such cases usually involved many different specialities and services, the clinic doctor perforce spent a lot of time checking on these other services' actions but could not *control* them. The way out of this dilemma was to set up another workshop, an integrated unit to take over the comprehensive assessment and management of some of the more complicated cases by involving community health, social work, therapies, etc. all under one roof. In such a manner the network of services increase.

Typically then, different settings were referred different clienteles and consequently dealt with a restricted range of identities.

Social identities

The social identities on offer in the different settings were basically of six major types arranged along a continuum of medical doubt about the child's health status. The relationship between clinical definitions and social identities was not isomorphic. Thus, the degree of medical doubt surrounding identities refers to the clinical condition's implications for either swamping other identities or at least creating difficulties for the assumption of other identities. For example, spina bifida as a clinical condition has differential identity implications depending on the extent to which it interferes with, for example, education, mobility, domestic organization, intellectual and social competence. Some spina-bifida children were 'impaired/remediable' while others were 'totally spoiled'. Similarly, epilepsy may be 'chronic', but 'not impairing' or 'chronic and spoiling' depending on severity. The main issue though is still the same. It is the doctor who translates the clinical identity into an 'appropriate' social identity. How that translation was made varied from setting to setting, as we have seen.

The identities which we are talking about cross-cut all clinical conditions; consequently, it must be made clear we are *not* talking about the content of clinical decision-making itself but instead of its socially organised consequences. Thus, Bloor's analysis of the clinical context of decision making in ENT children's out-patients does not deal with socially organized consequences of the activity of differentiation between those operated upon and those not; presumably the identities on offer in these clinics would be 'normal', 'abnormal-tolerable', and 'transient sick' with consequently limited biographical implications (Bloor 1978).

These identities can perhaps best be displayed diagrammatically.

Figure *Medical doubt and social identity*

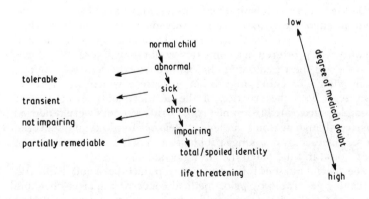

Typically, different settings dealt with different arrays of these identities. Local authority screening was concerned with 'normal' and 'tolerable abnormality', the special neurological clinic with problems felt by doctors to be 'chronic', 'impairing', and 'spoiling'. General clinics were concerned mainly with 'transient sickness' or 'chronic non-impairing' conditions. The special nursery and its follow-up clinic were concerned with 'transient' or 'continuing illness', the maternity hospital with the whole spectrum of identities and the therapies with 'chronic impairing', 'spoiling', or 'remediable' conditions.

However, displaying the identities as a flow chart should not be seen as implying that an unproblematic sorting procedure was followed in each setting. As we have aruged each major type of medical work presented different problems in managing the medical encounter; for example in establishing the health status of the child the doctor was, in differing degrees, dependent on the child or parent.

Thus, in the special nursery we noted that separation of the child from the mother enabled the doctors to impose and sustain a clinical framework in which the child's identity was a purely technical one, a set of biophysical properties that were generated by medicine's treatment concerns. The segregation allowed a collegial structure and, as the work was done in the absence of a parental audience, no deference had to be shown to the child's other potential identities. The points at which the clinical world and the parental world coincided, the mother's visits, and contacts with staff, were doubt-inducing, indicating that the child required further medical surveillance although most were expected to be 'normal'.

On the maternity hospital wards, screening as we have seen was done in such a way as to limit involvement of the mother while affirming that the child was normal enough. But, the normal identity was proffered in a context of doubt — why screen if all was well — and the threatening clinical agenda was routinely hidden from view. Teaching and other features, which might have interfered with the creation of the normal identity were where possible segregrated from the task at hand. Mothers were rendered passive, though anxious, audiences. Reasons for doubt if uncovered were remedied by invoking specialists in repair and reconstruction that would in time make the child normal enough.

The special nursery follow-up clinic on the other hand dealt with screening generated by prior medical concern and, after checking all was as well as it was expected to be, the child was constituted as normal and parental doubt sought and eliminated. The standard checklist provided an immutable clinic order although as doubt had been great so normalization was also great.

The Local Authority clinics' screening again took place against a presumption of normality that was ritually confirmed. But, due to the marginality of the doctors the tendency was to more narrow screening to conform to legitimate medical limits than in fact was intended. Reform or education were therefore rather rare, as such attempts took place in a context of precarious medical authority in the existing division of labour. Attendance was voluntary and parents were treated with *courtesy*, their answers to any questions that implied checking were almost invariably honoured. Parents were treated as caring, concerned, and dutiful and their children as wayward as any normal child would be.

In receptive settings, such as the general clinic, the work done conformed more closely to the traditional model of patient-practitioner contact; client-initiated for specialist adjudication. Such work again took place in a context of a presumption of normality but as there was a presenting problem the work of the doctor was devoted to the elimination of a state of illness. Such elimination was done in an interrogative fashion with elaborate checks to establish the data needed to definitively pronounce an illness or its absence. Such work never implied or raised the issue of normality. Where such doubt did exist it occurred in two forms: one where 'maintenance' of 'tolerable' illness/abnormality required the child should not be allowed to drift into the handicapped category, and the other where doubt existed but was not directly addressed but encouraged through elongation of time spans and refusal to validate the child as definitively 'well'.

In the special clinic the child was seriously in doubt and elaborate and meticulous checking, repeated recalls, and refusal to make definite prognoses served to increase that doubt. Parents were held awaiting the opportune moment when they would indicate acceptance of the identity delayed/handicapped. 'Telling' was a difficult business for it moved the doctor out of the security of traditional medical work and into counselling and management roles where the doctor did not directly control all the relevant services but instead 'checked' that they were being used to full advantage. In this setting the emergent 'working consensus' was fragile and subject to considerable buffeting as parents changed their views of the child's competences. Normalizing was absent and the doctor sought to enlist the parents as aides in his efforts at managing the handicapped child. Parents grew progressively 'wiser' over time and more trusted by the doctor. An accommodating relationship was sought and often established, but over a long period of time.

The therapies were again insulated against parents as audiences for their work, but dependent on parts for home continuation of their therapy programmes. But, in therapy co-operation was also required from the child, so as well as a clinical format and identity the therapists also had to produce 'characters' and a game format for the child to allow them to judge the extent to which the clinics either could or would engage in purposeful therapy. 'Progress' was offered to the parents but was limited to *therapeutic* progress, not overall progress. Pronouncements on overall progress entailed a judgement on the essential nature of the child and that was something that only doctors could provide.

In all the settings there was the potential for children to be accorded the 'wrong' identity by parents. This was most noticeable in the maternity wards, the special nursery follow-up clinic, and in the 'maintenance' cases of the general clinics and the special neurological clinic. It was at these crucial branching points that a variety of doubt-removing and doubt-producing procedures were used. There were not just verbal cues but also general demeanour when faced with the child. From this I think we can see just how restricted in focus the literature on 'communication' is.

As we noted in Chapter 2 most of the doctor's communicative efforts were directed at parents rather than at the children. In establishing the child's identity the doctor did not have to convince the child, but to convince its parents. This was a rather more difficult job than convincing the child. Children are relatively powerless, they do not write history books nor theorize about the way they wish to be viewed or valued. A history of childhood is a history written by adults interpreting children's actions and intentions from an adult perspective. They are, therefore, ready prey for adults' wider social claims and usages. For example, the 'psychogenic' approach to the history of childhood is not one that will ever be deemed contestable by children but will be refuted by other adults (de Mause 1974).

Childhood can be used to support adult claims about the harshness of the past and the enlightenment of the present or vice versa (Ariès 1963). Either way, the protagonists are adults using 'childhood' to point to a glorious state of nature lost to adults, or the oppressiveness of industrial civilization. Where children are granted 'rights' as a distinct group, these 'rights' are to be exercised by adults on their behalf (Court 1976). Perforce, medical work with children is really medical work with their parents or parental surrogates. As adults they can legitimately and are expected to enter the arena where the child's health status is in doubt. As we have argued, whether or not their claims are validated depends on their place in a hierarchy of other adults, and on their credibility when subjected to medical scepticism.

What we have tried to show in the various chapters is the way in which settings, clientele, and doctors' methods of constituting the child in public as having a particular identity cohere in typical combinations, and the ways in which the child's identity is provided for the parent. We also noted that overt challenges to such medical formulations were rare events. Not surprisingly it was at points when most was at stake, when the parents were being proffered a discredited and impaired identity for their child that challenges were more overt, where consensus was fragile and subject to periodic assault. For the most part, though, the doctor's translation of the child's clinical state into a social identity proved, overtly at least, successful. Parents appeared willing to accept what the doctor offered. We have no data on those who dropped out of contact and it would be instructive to know why some did appear to vote with their feet and refuse further specialist contact. It may well be that for these parents the clinical perspective and parents social perspective were strikingly at odds (Mercer 1972). In a highly centralized health-care system those that do not accept can only withdraw, for shopping around is not encouraged. In this case then we should be careful about generalizing — the clients that we saw apparently accepting the doctor's diagnosis may have been only those adjusting to the clinics proffered social indentities, while those unable or unwilling to adjust may well have dropped out of formal medical contact. An observational study will of course miss these important limiting cases.

Medical dominance

The issue of doctors' 'dominance' we have shown to be more complex than e.g. Freidson allows (Freidson 1970). Doctors' direct authority ended at clinic doors, the legitimacy of their medical work (i.e. the extent to which it can mobilize features such as expertise, autonomy, an engineering model) was in some cases precarious e.g. the Local Authority doctors' screening services. In all cases, to be sure, doctors initiated most conversation, but the relationship between doctors and their clients was modified by the degree of doubt, type of work, and setting. Enforcement or direct orders in most cases were eschewed as was any systematic involvement in family life. Instead, a circumscribed role was adopted, one that conformed more closely to what we have elsewhere termed 'bureaucratic medicine' (Strong and Davis 1978). In the special clinic we noted an awkward process of accommodation and acceptance of the limits of medicine and the doctor adopting a co-ordinating, checking, and counselling role — altogether more passive than we might expect from Freidson's analysis. Where parents were long-time attenders, had information that the doctor required, were responsible for the home management of the child, then doctors tended to surrender more clinic control. What else could they do except to provide a sympathetic ear and exert such control over other services as they could on their clients' behalf. This is not to argue that doctors' dominance was therefore removed. It was tempered and modified by the clientele and setting in which they worked. To be sure, as we have seen, doctors remained in control throughout; client revolts were rare. They controlled important resources such as expert knowledge, they controlled what was to count as 'medical' and 'not medical', access to their setting (but in different degree), the focus of interaction in settings, the medical notes and records, they had the right to ask questions and expect answers. However, as we have argued, these somewhat general features of medical dominance were modified in practice. Where, for example, the clients were presumed normal, attendance was voluntary, where the legitimacy of the initiative mode was weak, sharp imposition and demonstration of doctor control would probably serve to destroy the fragile relationship. The same applied where no cures could be offered, where doctors did not control access to necessary resources, where bad news was to be conveyed and a relationship sought and maintained — again imposition of sharp control was deemed inappropriate. Instead, greater rights were ceded to the parents to shape and control the content of the interaction.

Nevertheless, Freidson's general point on medical dominance is taken. This dominance and control works in a number of different ways as we have seen. It works through the general diffusion and acceptance of the legitimacy of medicine as an activity, through the creation and acceptance of moral obligations connected with illness in the sick role, through the legitimation in individual encounters of the ideology of medicine as a superior, specialized activity within a special domain of life called ill health. It occurs through medicine's links with science as a more general ideology characterized by certain proven knowledge, rationality, instrumentalism, universalism, and neutrality. A result of this is another feature that runs throughout the chapters in this book, the ways in which medicine affirms a 'natural' order of society, the naturalness of the family as a unit, that women will of course know more about children than men, that mothers' duties and responsibilities are 'natural' and spring from normal motives, that children make a family, and so on. In short, medicine seems to stress the world as it is and its naturalness and even necessity, not how it should be or might be. The ways in which medicine is involved in providing validation and certification for exemptions from social roles or access to desired facilities also places medicine in a strategic position. All of these worked to promote interaction in clinics that was patterned and stable, as for the most part the parents also seemed to accept that this was the way the world should be. This is not to argue that doctors' dominance was unlimited. Indeed, the main argument has been that they are in various ways subject to the controls of their work settings, the nature of their clientele, the position of their work settings in the wider division of labour, and so on. General dominance is thus tempered by the occasions in which it is used.

Finally, to go right back to the beginning, there is the issue of medical work. In working through the chapters, it should be clear by now that the observation done in the Scottish City child health system would tend to endorse Freidson's comments on studies of doctors and patients. Possibly too much attention has been given to the study of characteristics of doctors and characteristics of patients and not enough to the contexts of medical practice. There is now a substantial literature that documents the global differences between health care systems in, for example the USA, the UK, and other countries in respect of finance, distribution of resources, and types and organization of health care services. We also know a considerable amount about differences in health and illness beliefs and action. What is still missing are studies that throw a little more light on the circumstances of practice. Freidson's point is well taken that 'the level of technical performance, the approach to the client, "cynicism" and ethicality, do not vary so much with the individual's formal training as with the social setting in which he works' (Freidson 1970: 89-90). Hopefully, further comparative studies of medical work with children will throw more light on these issues than has been possible in this short monograph.

Appendix
The Research

Research projects vary in the extent to which they are dependent on the world they are studying. At one extreme we can perhaps talk about 'independent' research and at the other 'contingent' research. At the 'independent' extreme we can place projects that manufacture their own reality for study, they best example being the experimental situation in which research subjects are brought together under researcher-created conditions into a controlled environment in which they are insulated from the contaminating effects of prior social structure, and in which they are captive and controlled subjects available for study by rigorous scientific manipulation of pretested instruments. This natural science model *par excellence* is one to which much sociology aspires in its intense preoccupation with methodology. There is, however, a gap between a researcher's aspirations and the execution of most projects, which are in fact rather less 'independent'. The gap is remedied by other techniques, correct sampling, statistical manipulation, tested instruments, methods of coping with 'biasses', low response rates, etc., all brought about by the sociologist having to face a more intractable population who may not wish to be interviewed, who give ambiguous responses, and so on. In such circumstances, the attraction of 'captive' samples is obvious; they are total, controlled, predictable, and available. But the problem with such 'captive' samples is that they have been created not by the researcher for his purposes, but by others with often very different purposes in mind, e.g. to lock them up, police them, or treat them. The use of such samples for generalization about, for example, family structure or psychological profiles, is dubious, to say the least. The name is of course true of officially produced statistics that mirror the concerns of those collecting them rather than those of the researcher using them (Kitsuse and Cicourel 1963).

At the other end of the spectrum we have what we have called 'contingent' research. Typically, such research is dependent in a number of ways on its objects of study and faces rather different problems. Perhaps the most extreme case is that of the anthropological ethnography, which is heavily dependent on its object of study. Typically there are problems of locating the object of study (the tribe may have moved since last sighted), of gaining entry to locales, of gaining access to informants (who may be more or less reliable and have various axes to grind), of steering a judicious political path through attempts at incorporation into various factions and so on, as Wax so graphically describes (Wax 1971). At any point the research endeavour can be blocked by all kinds of unpredictable situational exigencies (e.g. getting ejected, political changes) and is continually conditional research. Typical methods that cluster with this polar type are a commitment to naturalistic enquiry, 'insightful' work, participant observation, and the collection of qualitative data in which the recorder demonstrably has a part in its production. Rather than arbitrarily isolating certain characteristics for manipulation the approach seeks to 'understand' the situated problematics of the group's existence through daily contact (however unlikeable the tribe might be). Typically such work is 'artful', and doesn't seem to 'fit' easily with the natural science model at all. For example there is always the danger that the researcher may have 'gone native', i.e. become indistinguishable from the object of study.'

Other forms of sociological enquiry also 'suffer' from the vicissitudes of the real world. Thus, longitudinal, career, and prospective designs are contingent on their social context remaining the same for their successful outcome, cohorts should not die en masse, people should not be so geographically mobile as to be untraceable, new organizational arrangements should not intervene to add new hazards to sample designs, the original 'guesswork' that goes into setting up prospective designs should be able to encompass the 'drift' that invariably occurs whenever the object of study is itself changing, emergent, or a process which by its nature forces the researcher to follow it wherever it goes. 'Natural' experiments are just such 'contingent' studies and consequently suffer the buffets that the real world hands out to all sociologists who venture away from the safety of the cross-sectional, one-shot survey technique — the safest we have.

Not surprisingly, perhaps, wherever possible sociologists have gone for the most 'independent' types of research methods, and for those slices of life that seem to lend themselves to 'independent' study. The use of such methods is, however, differentially applied in the different fields of sociology.

Thus, while for example researchers in fertility, criminology, social class, and medical sociology seem typically to employ 'independent' methods, other fields seem to display greater variation in their dominant methodological paradigms. Thus, case studies of deviant subcultures, organizational processes and work groups, and ethnographic studies can be found in greater profusion in the areas of deviance, organizational and industrial sociology, and community studies.

One might suggest that 'contingent' research has greater legitimacy as an enterprise and indeed is seen as the proper way in which research should be conducted in these fields. An uninvestigated topic (and one that we shall also ignore in this monograph) is the way in which dominant methodological paradigms emerge in the different fields of sociology over time, and the way in which future researchers' endeavour is directed by the different traditions in the different areas. Some attempts to get to grips with this as a topic can be found at a theoretical level in analysis of 'schools' of sociology, but to my knowledge no-one has ever attempted to chart the rise and fall of methodological paradigms within particular fields of sociology.

The research reported in this monograph falls at the 'contingent' end of the continuum we have described. In this sense it is committed to 'naturalistic' enquiry and is dependent on the world that it studies. It began as a study of the impact of a new form of medical organization on pre-existing forms of medical organization. In this sense it was a before and after study, a study of a 'natural' experiment. But like all 'natural' experiments, the decisions of those creating the new organization, in effect creating the conditions for the 'natural' experimental situation, were not under the control of the researcher. The *outcome* of the 'experiment' was unpredictable, despite its embodiment in the architectural plans as bricks and mortar in a defined location. This was the research question.

Slightly less unpredictable was the target population for the new organization. Here we were guided by medical opinion as to the likely source of clients for the new organization and consequently sought and gained entry to the major hospital out-patient clinic that currently handled the bulk of what was thought to be the new organization's likely cases. There, we waited for the organization to open in order to look at the differences in medical practice that the new organization made.

We also intended to interview parents of children who attended the 'old' clinic and those who attended the 'new' one and hoped that some, a small proportion of 'old' clinic patients, would be transferred to the new one so that we could get parents' comparative experiences of the 'new' and the 'old'.

So far, so good. But the new organization failed to open on schedule due to a building strike, central government intervention, financial cuts, and hard winters, all, we felt, outside the control of the researchers. The ever-lengthening 'before' stage also allowed other structural features to impinge in the research, e.g. personnel changes in all departments concerned with the new organization and increasing indeterminacy in the distribution of knowledge about the future and functions of the new organization as 'key' personnel moved.

With no firm opening date, interviewing parents seemed rather hazardous as the population for the 'new' organization still had not been definitely identified by either the medical and educational personnel involved or the researchers. After a year or so a further set of constraints began to impinge — the exigencies of the funding process. Here we were lucky to be part of a programme grant that allowed us a flexibility of timing and execution that more formal funding does not usually allow. The SSRC accepted our apologetic annual reports on the 'drift' that had occurred. Even so, funds run out and faced with this prospect, of a 'before' but no 'after', we decided that we had to refocus the research while retaining as much of our already gathered material as possible.

Consequently, we sought and obtained access to other settings within the medical services where children were seen, and turned the research round to a comparative cross-sectional focus, comparing the work done in different settings with child in different degrees of doubt, a study of professional/client interaction.

A lot is made of the 'problems of access' in the literature which is available on 'contingent' methodology. In fact, we experienced very little difficulty. Our presence was unobtrusive; at most we asked for formal interviews at some stage, but in the main our presence was not seen as particularly damaging or dangerous. In this we were aided by the fact that in most of the settings we observed, audiences of neophytes were expected. In one, a special clinic, they were not encouraged, but our non-medical status meant we could be ignored — we did not 'require' teaching. On the basis of our experience we would say that access is perhaps overstressed as a problem. What worried us and made us uneasy was the periodic feeling that something important might be happening in another place in the medical services. Consequently, we extended our settings to encompass as many as we could manage. In retrospect, this feeling was probably illusory — not doubt most researchers in organizations get paranoid at times, feel excluded, and wonder if the 'real' action is not elsewhere and being denied them. We learnt to tolerate this — mainly because the doctors and other staff we came into contact with also at times displayed the same feelings. Probably it is a ubiquitous feature of a front-line organization.

This extension of our activities also provided us with a useful bonus; we were able in most settings to observe a number of different practitioners in action. Given the rhetoric of individualism in clinical practice we expected there to be considerable variation in style. In fact, by comparison, we were able to note the similarity in style of practitioners faced with similar tasks to perform. In this sense, the turnover in staff noted earlier proved accidentally useful in enabling us to observe different doctors dealing with the same types of cases under similar conditions.

The settings we observed were as follows:

(1) A special neurological clinic; 517 consultants observed; 218 'cases'; two doctors.
(2) General outpatient medical clinics: 67 consultants; 67 cases; two doctors.
(3) Ward rounds on a special nursery for the newborn: approximately forty babies were in the ward at any one time; staff varied too — six and upwards.
(4) Paediatric ward rounds in a maternity hospital: total population not known; number of consultations observed approximately seventy-five; two doctors.
(5) Local Authority children's clinics: 102 consultations; 105 cases; five doctors.
(6) Occupational and physiotherapy: 117 consultations; fifty-six cases; six therapists.
(7) A follow-up clinic of 'At Risk' children: twenty-seven consultations; twenty-seven cases; one doctor.
(8) A similar spectrum of clinics in a private USA hospital for handicapped children. The USA material has been excluded from the analysis because of the researchers' unfamiliarity with the USA system, the different meanings of practice generated by the payment system, the promotional and deliberate patient recruitment work done by doctors and the hospital, and the lack of an analogous 'field' of settings like the UK. These differences form the basis for further analysis which is not appropriate here simply due to health

care assumptions and structure. The 'strangeness' however
cast a useful perspective on our own cultural assumptions.

Our objective was to compare the work done in these different
settings which had in common children as their clients but varied in
the manner in which the work was directed at underlying
pathology. Our chosen methods for investigation were observation
and interview and comparison done wherever possible by the
researchers together or alternately in order to check each other's
observations. Typically we would sit in the clinic and write notes on
what was said, to be written up in detail later on. At one stage, to try
and produce verbatim transcripts, we attempted to split the
recordings, one writing the doctors' comments and the other the
parent/child's to 'merge' them later. While producing more data it
also produced more ambiguity — some bits we could not
synchronize and our verbal data is therefore partial. A tape-
recorder would no doubt have got round these difficulties. But
tape-recording would have been obtrusive in most of the settings,
particularly ward rounds, and would no doubt have seriously
impeded the doctor's work by the self-consciousness induced by
introducing yet another 'audience'. Consequently, despite its
deficiencies, note-taking was preferred. We were able to interview
some of the staff we observed, though with others it proved
unnecessary as there was ample time for doctors and others to
comment on the action and swap anecdotes with us. Doctors felt we
did not interfere with them; rather we were just background
features in the settings, welcome often as persons to chat to when
trade was slack.

References

Ariès, P. (1963) *Centuries of Childhood*. London: Penguin Books.

Arluke, A. (1980) Roundsmanship: Inherent Control on a medical teaching ward. *Social Science and Medicine* **14A**(4): 297-307.

Ball, D.L. (1967) An abortion clinic ethnography. *Social Problems* **14** (3): 293-301.

Barnes, K. and Stark, A. (1975) The Denver Developmental Screening Test. *American Journal of Public Health* **65**(4): 363—69

Becker, H. (163) *Outsiders*. Illinois: Free Press.

Berry, J. (1972) *Social Work with Children*. London: Routledge and Kegan Paul.

Blaxter, M. (1976) *The Meaning of Disability*. London: Heinemann.

Bloor, M. (1976) Bishop Berkeley and the adenotonsillectomy enigma. *Sociology* **10**(1): 43-61.

———— (1978) On the routinized nature of work in people processing agencies: the case of adeno-tonsillectomy assessment in ENT outpatient clinics. In A. Davis (ed.) (1978).

Bloor, M. and Gill, D. (1972) Screening the well child. *Community Medicine:* 24 November.

Bloor, M. and Horobin, G. (1975) Conflict and conflict resolution in doctor-patient interaction. In C. Cox and A. Mead (eds) *A Sociology of Medical Practice*. London: Macmillan.

Blum, A. and Rosenberg, L. (1968) Some problems involved in professionalizing social interaction: the case of psycho-therapeutic training. *Journal of Health and Social Behaviour* **9**(1): 72-85.

Byrne, P. and Long, B. (1976) *Doctors Talking to Patients*. London: HMSO.

Campbell, J. (1975) Attribution of illness another double standard? *Journal of Health and Social Behaviour* **16**(1): 114-26.

Chisholm, R. (1979) When should the state take over? *Legal Services Bulletin* **4**(4): 133-38.

Cartwright, A. and O'Brien, M. (1976) Social class variations in health care and in the nature of general practitioner consultations. In M. Stacey (ed.) (1976) *Sociology of the NHS*. Keele: Sociological Review Monograph No. 22.

Cicourel, A. and Kitsuse, J. *The Educational Decision Makers*. Indianapolis: Bobbs Merrill.

Conrad, P. (1979) Types of Medical Social Control *Sociology of Health and Illness* 1(1): 1-11.

Court Report (1976) *Fit for the Future*. Cmnd 6684. London: HMSO.

Daniels, A (1969) The Captive Professional Bureaucratic Limitations in the Practice of Military Psychiatry. *Journal of Health and Social Behaviour* 10(4): 255-65.

Danziger, S. (1978) The uses of expertise in doctor and patient encounters during pregnancy. *Social Science and Medicine* 12(5A) 359-67.

Davies, C. (1979) Organization Theory and the Organization of Health Care. *Social Science and Medicine* 13A, (4) 413-22.

Davis, A. (ed.) (1978) *Relationships Between Doctors and Patients*. Farnborough, Hants: Saxon House.

Davis, A. and Strong, P. (1975) The management of a therapeutic encounter. In M. Wadsworth and D. Robinson (eds) *Studies in Everyday Medical Life*. London: Martin Robertson.

—— (1976) Aren't children wonderful? A study of the allocation of identity in developmental assessment. In M. Stacey (ed.) *Sociology of the NHS*. Keele: Sociological Review Monograph No. 22.

Davis, F. (1963) *Passage Through Crisis*. New York Bobbs Merrill.

—— (1966) Uncertainty in medical prognosis. In F. Scott and W.R. Volkart (eds) *Medical Care*. New York: Wiley.

de Mause, L. (1974) *The History of Childhood*. New York: Souvenir Press.

Dingwall, R. and Eckelar, J. (1978) Social perceptions of child neglect. Paper given at 9th World Congress of Sociology: Uppsala 1978.

Duff, R. and Campbell, A. (1973) Moral and ethical dilemmas in the special care nursery. *New England Journal of Medical* 289(17): 890-94.

Ehrenreich, B. and English, D. (1979) *For Her Own Good, 150 years of experts' advice to women*. London: Pluto Press.

Emerson, J. (1970) Behaviour in Private Places. In H.P. Dreitzel (ed.) Recent Sociology No.2, *Patterns of Communicative Behaviour*. New York: Collier Macmillan.

Emerson, R. (1969) *Judging Delinquents*. New York: Aldine.

Foucault, M. (1973) *The Birth of the Clinic*. London: Tavistock.

Frankenberg, W., Camp, B.W., van Natta, P.A., Demerssemen, J. (1971) Reliability and stability of the Denver Developmental

Developmental Screening Test.*Child Development* **42**(5): 1313-125.

Freidson, E. (1970) *Profession of Medicine: A Study of the Sociology of Applied Knowledge.* New York: Dodd, Mead & Co.

Garfinkel, H. (1956) The Conditions of Successful Degradation Ceremonies. *American Journal of Sociology* **61**(5): 420-24.

Gibson, H. (1978) The dressings clinic in accident and emergency. In A. Davis (ed.) *Relationships Between Doctors and Patients.* Farnborough Hants: Saxon House.

Goffman, E. (1956) *The Presentation of Self in Everyday Life.* Edinburgh: Social Science Research Centre.

——— (1961a) Role distance. In E. Goffman *Encounters.* Indianapolis: Bobbs Merrill.

——— (1961b) The Medical Model and Mental Hospitalization: Some notes on the vicissitudes of the tinkering trades. In E. Goffman *Asylums.* New York: Anchor.

——— (1961c) *Asylums.* New York: Anchor.

——— (1978) *Gender Advertisements.* London: Macmillan.

Hall, D. (1978) *Social Relations and Innovation.* London: Routledge & Kegan Paul.

Holgate, E. (ed.) (1972) *Communicating with Children.* London: Longman.

Hoyles, M. (ed.) (1979) *Changing Childhood.* London: Writers and Readers Publishing Co-operative.

Hughes, E. (1958) *Men and Their Work.* Illinois: Free Press.

Illich, I. (1976) *The Limits of Medicine.* London: Marion Boyars.

Jewson, N. (1976) The Disappearance of the Sick Man from Medical Cosmology 1770-1870. *Sociology* **10**(3): 225-44.

Kitsuse, J. and Cicourel, A. (1963) A note on the uses of official statistics. *Social Problems* **11**(2): 131-39.

Lemert, E. (1967) *Human Deviance, Social Problems and Social Control.* New Jersey: Prentice Hall.

McHugh, P. (1970) A Commonsense perception of deviance. In H.P. Dreitzel (ed.) 1970 Recent Sociology No.2: *Patterns of Communicative Behaviour.* New York: Collier Macmillan.

Macintyre, S. (1977) *Single and Pregnant.* London: Croom Helm.

——— (1978) Obstetric Routines in Ante-Natal Care. In A. Davis, (ed.) *Relationships between Doctors and Patients.* Farnborough, Hants: Saxon House.

Mackay, R. (1973) Conceptions of children and models of socialization. In H.P. Dreitzel (ed.) Recent Sociology No.5 *Childhood and Socialization.* New York: Collier Macmillan.

McKeown, T. (19,ó) A historical appraisal of the medical task. In G. McLachlan and T. McKeown (eds) *Medical History and Medical Care.* London: Nuffield Provincial Hospitals Trust.

Mechanic, D. (1962) The sources of power of lower participants. *Administrative Science Quarterly* **7**(3): 349-64.

Mennerick, L. (1974) Client typologies: a method of coping with conflict in service worker-client relationship. *Sociology of Work and Occupations* **1**(4): 396-418.

Mercer, J. (1972) Who is normal? Two perspectives on mild mental retardation. In E.G. Jaco (ed.) *Patients, Physicians and Illness.* Illinois: Free Press.

Mitchell, R. (ed.) (1970) *Child Life and Health.* London: Longman.

Parmalee, A.J. (1962) European neurological studies of the newborn. *Child Development* **33**: 169-80.

Parsons, T. (1951) *The Social System* (Chapter 10). Chicago: Free Press.

Roberts, C.J. (1970) Developmental and neurological sequelae of the common complications of pregnancy and birth. *British Journal of Preventive Social Medicine* **24**(1): 33-8.

Robinson, D. (1971) *The Process of Becoming 11.* London: Routledge & Kegan Paul.

Rose, N. (1979) The psychological complex: mental measurement and social administration. *Ideology and Consciousness* **5**(Spring): 5-68.

Rosengren, W. and Devault, S. (1963) The sociology of time and space in an obstetric hospital. In E. Freidson (ed.) *The Hospital in Modern Society.* New Jersey: Free Press.

Roth, J. (1963) *Timetables.* Indianapolis: Bubbs-Merrill.

Rushing, W. (1964) *The Psychiatric Professions.* Chapel Hills: University of North Carolina Press.

Scheff, T. (1966) *Being Mentally Ill.* London: Weidenfeld.

———— (1968) Negotiating Reality. Notes on power in the assessment of responsibility. *Social Problems* **16**(1): 3-17.

Scott, M. and Lyman, S. (1968) Accounts. *American Sociological Review* **33**(1): 46-62.

Scott, R. (1968) *The Making of Blind Men.* New York: Russell Sage.

Stimson, G. and Webb, B. (1976) *Going to See the Doctor.* London: Routledge & Kegan Paul.

Strong, P. (1980) *The Ceremonial Order of the Clinic.* London: Routledge & Kegan Paul.

Strong, P. and Davis, A. (1977) Role, Role Formats and Medical Encounters. *Sociological Review* **25**(4): 775-800.

———— (1978) Who's Who in Paediatric Encounters. In A. Davis (ed.) *Relationships Between Doctors and Patients.* Farnborough, Hants: Saxon House.

Sundnow, D. (1967) *Passing On.* New Jersey. Prentice Hall.

Tuckett, D. (1977) *An Introduction to Medical Sociology.* London:

Tavistock.

Voysey, M. (1975) *A Constant Burden*. London: Routledge & Kegan Paul.

Waddington, I. (1973) The role of the hospital in the development of modern medicine. *Sociology* **7**(2): 211-24.

Waitzkin, H. and Stoeckle, J. (1972) The Communication of information about illness: clinical, sociological and methodological considerations. *Advances in Psychosomatic Medicine* **8**: 180-215.

Wax, R. (1971) *Doing Fieldwork*. Chicago: University of Chicago Press.

Wenar, C. and Coulter, J. (1962) A reliability study of developmental histories. *Child Development* **33**: 453-62.

Woodmonsey A.C. (1917) Parent guidance. *Developmental Medicine and Child Neurology* **13**: 243-44.

Wright, H.J. (1969) The present role of the GP in the medical care of children. *British Journal of Medical Education* **3**: 269-76.

Name Index

Subject Index

abnormality 14: handicapped identity 105-06, 122, 125, 137, 160-61; normalizing of, 70-3, 105; *see also* normality; special clinics
abortion 10
access problems 167
advice 46, 52-3, 56, 59, 97, 154
affirmation of normality 78-83
age of child 32, 66, 106-07, 133
agenda: 'hidden' 117; of special clinic 107-08
aides, parents as 54, 109, 111-14, 120-21, 126, 137
ambiguity 90-1, 93, 96, 100, 123
amusement *see* joking; wonder
appointment, time allowed, 11-12, 85, 88, 95, 106
assessment: and doubts 108-13, 126-37; of parents 113-21
at-risk register 41, 141

'bad news', telling 108, 121-26
behaviour of children 28-37, 55; in special clinics 108-13, 127, 132-33; in therapy 149-52
'body maintenance' work 57

care, residential 131-32
central administration 40-3
check: in general clinic 95-102; in initiative medicine 63-6, 74-6; in special clinic 129; 'standard' 63-6
children: age of 32, 66, 106-07, 133; as clinical objects 62-73, 140-45, 139-54; in clinics 21-39; excluded 22, 30-2; in general clinic 86-104, 158; incompetence of 13, 17-18, 22-7, 133, 139, 145; in Local Authority clinic 40-60, 158-59; management of 30-7; in maternity hospital 62-73, 158; normal childhood 37-9; in nursery follow-up clinic 73-84, 158; as performers 109-12; powerless 160; in special clinic 105-38, 158; in special nursery 140-45, 158; in therapy 145-54; walk-on role 89, 94; as work 139-54; *see also* abnormality; behaviour; normality; parents
childbirth 10, 64, 66
childhood 1, 13, 37-9
client-initiated contacts 14-15, 159
client-dependency 3, 5
clientele 14-16, 41-5
clinic: general 85-104, 158; Local Authority 40-60, 158-59; maternity hospital 62-73; nursery follow-up 61, 63, 73-84, 158; special 103-38, 158; special nursery 140-45, 158; therapy 145-54
clinical object, child as 62-73, 139-54
collegial structure 3, 62-73, 139-45 *passim*
constraints on doctors 40-1, 47-9
construction of normality 56-60
'contingent' research 164-66, 168
continuity, lack of 47
control of work 40-1, 62-3